BACK

TO FRUGAL

Transforming Your Money Habits for a Better Life

Kelly Fierce

TABLE OF CONTENTS

INTRODUCTION

In my late twenties, I stumbled upon the concept of frugality. Despite growing up with a strong work ethic instilled by my dad, I struggled with saving and often spent every dollar I earned. However, things started to shift after college when I began dating someone from a wealthy yet incredibly frugal family. Initially, I had misconceptions about what it meant to be frugal. I used to equate it with being stingy or always opting for the cheapest option. However, my ex's family showed me a different perspective. Despite their wealth, they didn't flaunt it with flashy cars or a lavish lifestyle. In fact, you wouldn't have guessed they were millionaires just by looking at them. They taught me invaluable lessons about saving money and living within one's means. Their approach sparked a transformation in how I managed my finances, setting me on a journey towards financial responsibility and long-term stability.

As I embraced a frugal lifestyle, I noticed a positive shift in my financial situation: my debts began to decrease, and my savings started to grow. While this happened, I saw many of my friends continuing to live as if they were affluent, indulging in big homes, fancy cars, and designer clothes. However, behind this facade of wealth, they were actually accumulating expensive loans and accruing significant credit card debt. That's when I realized the difference between real wealth, not just the appearance of it. And if I wanted to have wealth, I had to ditch my debts and fully embrace a frugal lifestyle. This journey transformed my life, guiding me toward a more secure and prosperous future.

Frugal refers to the quality of being economical or thrifty in using resources, especially money. It involves avoiding unnecessary expenses and making wise and efficient choices to save and manage resources effectively. Living a frugal lifestyle is essential for breaking free from debt and building savings, especially amid economic challenges such as the pandemic.

In the wake of the 2020 financial turmoil sparked by the COVID-19 pandemic, our financial landscape experienced a significant transformation. This crisis brought unprecedented challenges to individuals and families across America. Jobs vanished, businesses faltered, and the everyday routines we took for granted were upended. The repercussions were felt in every household, from adapting to remote learning challenges to facing the strain of increased grocery bills.

The pandemic wasn't just a health crisis but a seismic shift that reshaped our jobs, finances, and lifestyle choices. Its impact transformed our daily lives in several ways:

1. Shifting Spending Habits: Lockdowns reshaped our spending habits, emphasizing essential goods, health expenses, and home-related investments.

2. Job Insecurity: Closures created widespread job insecurity, prompting many to rethink the stability of their careers.

3. Skill Development Focus: Adapting to a changing job market, people invested time and effort in learning new skills to enhance their employability.

4. Rise of Side Hustles: Job uncertainties led to the exploration of alternative income sources, fostering the growth of side hustles and entrepreneurship.

5. Financial Awareness: Economic uncertainty heightened financial awareness, leading individuals to prioritize emergency savings, reduce debt, and adopt frugal spending habits.

The pandemic highlighted the need for improved money management in the U.S. Mastering effective money management is a self-taught journey. It doesn't necessarily require a college degree, as mastering money is less about intellect and more about behavior. In this changing landscape where job security is no longer guaranteed, being smarter about money is not an option; it's a necessity.

For too long, many Americans have been living beyond their means, frequently leaning on credit cards to sustain their lifestyle. It's critical to shift towards a frugal way of life in this post-pandemic era. Doing so promotes financial responsibility and lays the foundation for a more sustainable and secure future.

Being frugal involves making deliberate choices, cutting unnecessary expenses, and committing to saving diligently. It helps regain stability, build an emergency fund, and develop smart money management habits. By embracing frugality, individuals can break free from the cycle of debt, ensuring resilience in tough economic times. This book isn't a quick fix; it's a journey toward financial stability that starts with that first step.

It's time for us, as a society, to get back to being frugal.

CHAPTER 1

DEBT AND GOALS

Welcome to the first chapter where we tackle the nitty-gritty of debt and setting financial goals. In simple terms, debt is when you owe someone money. It's not a fun word, and it often brings stress along with it. Most people don't start with a debt problem; it usually sneaks up on them over time. Spending more than you earn is a common cause, and sadly, it's become a norm for many Americans. The COVID-19 pandemic acted as a wake-up call for many. With jobs disappearing and financial security crumbling, people were compelled to reevaluate their career choices and spending habits and devise alternative ways to pay their bills and debts.

Debt can be caused by reduced income, underestimating future expenses, divorce, poor money management, gambling, medical expenses, and more. It steals your financial freedom, making your lenders decide how you use your money. The kind, amount, and cost of the debt you take on can determine whether it's considered good or bad. Good debt examples include a reasonable student loan, an affordable mortgage, or a car loan for essential transportation. Low-interest debt that enhances your income or net worth is also considered good. However, excessive debt, regardless of the opportunities it may offer, can become bad debt.

Bad debt, which negatively impacts your financial situation, includes expensive debts with high or variable interest rates, particularly when used for non-essential expenses or depreciating items. Credit card debt can quickly go from manageable to burdensome, especially when a high-interest card starts racking up balances. While taking a personal loan for non-essential spending isn't recommended, using it wisely to pay off higher-interest debts like credit cards without reusing them can be a sensible choice. On the other hand, payday loans are an example of extremely bad debt, carrying exorbitant interest rates that make them immediately unaffordable. Their short-term nature often traps borrowers in a cycle of debt. Regardless of whether you consider debt good or bad, it's important to pay it off if you aim to build wealth.

Getting into debt is a bit like gaining weight. Initially, a few extra pounds from unhealthy eating habits might go unnoticed. Similarly, spending more than you earn and relying on credit cards can lead to financial trouble. Eventually, you realize you're deeper in debt than you'd like. Much like deciding to change habits for weight loss, tackling debt requires setting achievable goals. It's not about overthinking your future career but keeping it simple. Focus on becoming debt-free, estimate the time needed for each debt payoff, build an emergency savings plan, and outline the steps to get there. The key to eliminating debt lies in changing your financial habits and maintaining discipline. It takes time and effort, but securing a debt-free future is worth the journey, just like shedding those extra pounds.

To tackle debt, understanding your attitudes about money is critical. The pandemic underscored the need for emergency savings and financial resilience, pushing individuals to adopt more sensible financial practices and to spend more cautiously. Living frugally is pivotal to stay below your means and avoid the burden of debt. By spending wisely, prioritizing needs over wants, and saving money, you create financial stability, allowing you to achieve your goals and enjoy life without the stress of excessive debt.

CHAPTER 2

GETTING ORGANIZED

I n this chapter, we're diving into the importance of staying organized in your financial journey. Why? Because keeping things in order isn't just about tidiness—it's your ticket to paying bills on time, avoiding late fees, and maintaining a positive credit history. It contributes to a stress-free financial routine, reducing the risk of missed payments and financial setbacks. Being organized also facilitates budgeting, enabling you to allocate funds wisely, save for goals, and build a secure financial foundation.

There are several items that can help you get organized. Don't worry if you don't have some of these. It's optional if you want to buy them or use a few of the suggested frugal tactics.

1. Having a computer (or laptop), printer, and an email address is optional but convenient. It's not extremely important, but at some point, you may have to write a letter to a company, retrieve a document from a company to sign, or print resumes to send out. A frugal option is to use the printer at work or ask a friend who has one.

2. A Calendar: You can use your smartphone, but it may help to have an actual calendar to see the whole month at a glance and see any upcoming due dates for bills, appointments, or events. You can buy one or find a company that gives them out for free or print from home using the internet.

3. A USB flash drive (also called a thumb drive, jump drive, or memory stick): This is for storing important electronic documents such as files and photos.

4. A filing system: This could be a small accordion file or a file cabinet. This is to organize your bills and documents you may need to retrieve quickly.

5. A fireproof safe: This is a place to keep your most important documents, such as your passport, birth certificate, social security cards, diplomas, extra ATM or credit cards, car title, expensive jewelry, etc.

6. An address book: Sure, your smartphone might already have your contacts' addresses stored, but having them written down in an old-school address book can be a lifesaver in case you lose your phone. You can keep your address book in your fireproof safe as well.

7. A shredder: If you can't buy one, use your workplace shredder if available. A frugal option is to block out your information with a dark pen or marker and then use scissors

to cut up documents with your personal information and discard them in several trash bins. This helps prevent identity theft, which will be explained later.

8. A key rack: Hang a small key rack near your door to save time searching for misplaced keys. Consider placing another near your bedroom closet for extra keys. Use key chains with blank tags for labeling and a customized one with your name to help identify lost keys at a friend's place or work.

9. Post-it notes: These sticky notes are useful for jotting down important tasks or shopping items. You can also consider putting a dry-erase board on your fridge or simply using the Notes or Reminder section on your smartphone for a frugal alternative.

10. A Budget: Using a budget, whether on your smartphone or handwritten, is important to have. It helps track income, expenses, and savings goals, ensuring a clear understanding of your financial situation. We'll dive deeper into budgeting in a separate chapter.

11. A Bill Checklist: This list can be hand written or created in Excel and printed out. It helps you check off any bills you've paid, the amount, and any notes needed. I would use this every month to ensure that all your bills have been paid. See sample at the end of the book.

12. A calculator and checkbook: Balancing your checkbook is a breeze with a calculator. You can also use the one on your smartphone or computer for added convenience. With a checkbook, you can record every transaction, even pending purchases. When you write a check or make a debit card purchase, it might not immediately reflect in your bank balance. This delay can lead to confusion and potential overdrafts. However, by recording each transaction in your checkbook, you create a real-time ledger that prevents you from spending more than you have. If you don't use a checkbook, make sure to use the check register that comes with it (usually free from your bank). This handy register is your go-to guide for tracking when bills were paid, and how much was paid, and it can be a lifesaver if you ever need to dispute a payment with a company.

SAMPLE OF BILL CHECKLIST:

Example	Amount	Paid	Notes (can add date paid & how it was paid)
Rent	$1,000	X	Due 1st of month – paid early, Check sent on 12/15
Car Pymt	$ 300	X	Transferred online 1/1
Electric Bill	$ 75	X	Paid with Bill Pay on 1/1
Heating Bill	$ 75	X	Paid with Bill Pay on 1/1

Start by listing your important bills at the top, including the amount, and leaving a space for a checkmark. Check off each bill as you pay it, and note the typical payment date. This way, you'll be able to spot if a bill hasn't arrived within its usual timeframe, as bills can sometimes go missing in the mail. If paying all your bills at once feels inconvenient or strains your paycheck, consider calling your service providers. Explore the possibility of adjusting your bill due dates to better align with your financial schedule. For example, if your rent or mortgage due date was on the first of the month, then perhaps pay it early with your previous month's paycheck that was paid mid-month. This will allow you to free up your first month's paycheck toward other bills.

Put this bill checklist where you can see it daily, like on the fridge. This simple system helps you stay organized and avoids credit score troubles, a topic we'll delve into later.

SAMPLE OF USING A TRANSACTION REGISTER (CHECKBOOK)

Check #	Date	Description of Transaction	Payment/ Debit	Deposit	Balance
					$500.00
	1/1	Direct deposit – work		$2,000. 00	2500.00
#1	1/1	ABC Company for Rent	1000.00		1500.00
#2	1/1	Utility Bill	75.00		1425.00
#3	1/1	Daycare bill	500.00		925.00

	1/1	Gas (bought on Visa card)	50.00		**875.00**

For example, you started out with a balance of $500, then added your paycheck of $2,000, and then subtracted your bills and expenses as you paid them. Your realistic balance would now be **$875.00**. Some transactions, such as checks or payments made with your Debit card, which also acts as a Visa card, can take several days to get processed by your bank. For example, let's say Check #1 and #2 cleared with your bank, but Check #3 did not, and neither did the gas purchase. If you looked at your bank account online or over the phone, it may tell you that your balance is $1,425 dollars. But this is incorrect. It just means that some expenses/checks have not cleared through the bank yet. That's why it's important to use a transaction register to keep track of every expense that you make from your bank account. It will give you the true balance, which, in this sample, was $875.00 dollars, not $1,425.00 dollars. I'd also put a checkmark on each transaction that you know cleared through your bank.

Check #	Date	Description of Transaction	Payment/ Debit (-)	Deposit (+)	Balance
					$500.00
	11/14/23	√ Direct deposit – work		$2,000.00	2500.00

#1	11/15/23	√ ABC Company for Rent	1000.00		1500.00
#2	11/15/23	√ Utility Bill	75.00		1425.00
#3	11/15/23	Daycare bill	500.00		925.00
	11/15/23	Chevron – gas	50.00		**875.00**

Using a checkbook or transaction register isn't just about tracking spending; it's a tool for discipline and accountability. It makes you actively involved with your money, heightening awareness of your choices. Unlike swiping a credit card, it visually shows your bank balance decreasing with each expense, preventing overspending.

CHAPTER 3

LIST AND PAY

OFF DEBTS

I n Chapter 3, we delve into the essential task of understanding and managing your debts. This crucial step is pivotal for achieving financial stability. The process begins with creating a comprehensive list of all your debts, providing a clear picture of your financial obligations. This list should include credit cards, car loans, student loans, mortgages, and any outstanding balances, serving as a roadmap for debt reduction.

Once you've compiled your debt list, prioritizing how to tackle them becomes imperative. Two prominent strategies for debt repayment are the **avalanche method** and the **snowball method**.

The **avalanche method** prioritizes paying off debts with the highest interest rate first, saving money on interest payments. While it saves you more money in the long run, it might not give you the same feel-good vibes as the snowball method.

EXAMPLE USING THE AVALANCHE METHOD:

List all your debts, the balance you owe, and the interest rate on each one. Pay the minimum due on each debt and then put any extra money toward your highest interest rate debt (for example, Credit Card), despite the fact that the actual total amount of the student loan has the highest balance owed.   Sticking to the avalanche method demands unwavering belief in the process and persistent determination, qualities that may be challenging to sustain over the long run.

Type of Debt	Balance Owed	Interest Rate
Credit Card	$ 10,000.00	20 %
Student Loan	$12,000.00	6 %
Car Loan	$ 6,000.00	4 %
Total Debt	$28,000.00	

The **snowball method** involves paying off debts from smallest to largest balances, regardless of interest rates. In this same example, you would focus on paying the minimum balance due on each debt and then put any extra money toward the debt with the lowest balance owed (for example, the car loan).

EXAMPLE USING THE SNOWBALL METHOD:

Type of Debt	Balance Owed	Interest Rate	
Credit Card	$ 10,000.00	20 %	
Student Loan	$ 12,000.00	6 %	
Car Loan	$ 6,000.00	4 %	
Total Debt	$ 28,000.00		

This approach focuses on the psychological aspect of debt reduction, emphasizing quick wins by eliminating smaller debts first. This provides a sense of accomplishment, boosting motivation and confidence to tackle larger debts. Many people prefer this method because paying off debt is not just about numbers, it's also about emotions. Starting with smaller debts gives you a sense of control and achievement.

WHAT ARE SOME STEPS NOT TO TAKE WHEN PAYING OFF DEBT?

When you're working on getting out of debt, it's imperative to stop accumulating more debt – think of it like trying to lose weight by eating healthy and exercising, but then indulging in a bunch of junk food. Avoid taking out new credit lines to pay off existing debts. While using a home equity loan may seem tempting, it puts your home at risk. Borrowing from your 401(k) may incur high costs and double taxation, impacting your retirement savings. If you don't repay a 401(k) loan after leaving your job, it can result in penalties and taxes. Resist the urge to tap into your 401(k) and you'll be thankful once you retire.

WHAT IF YOU OWE MONEY TO FAMILY OR FRIENDS?

Prioritize repaying family or friends to maintain trust and relationships. Clearing IOUs ensures financial integrity and avoids strain on personal relationships. Prioritizing these repayments is key to preserving trust and financial stability.

WHAT IF YOU OWE MONEY TO THE IRS?

If you owe back taxes to the Internal Revenue Service (IRS), it's extremely important to prioritize paying back these types of financial obligations. Tackling your tax debt promptly helps prevent any further complications with the IRS.

WHAT IF YOU RECEIVE A WINDFALL?

If you suddenly receive a windfall of money (inheritance, insurance settlement, home sale, etc.), handle it wisely, especially if you have debts. First and foremost, prioritize paying off high-interest debts to relieve immediate financial pressure. Then, consider setting aside a portion of the money in a separate bank account for emergency savings. Seeking professional advice for long-term financial planning can also be beneficial.

Avoid the temptation of impulsive spending and instead focus on investments that offer returns. It's essential to exercise caution and avoid spending all the money quickly. Instead, adopt a smart and frugal mindset, aiming to save and invest wisely for a secure and debt-free future.

CHAPTER 4

BUDGET BASICS

Welcome to Chapter 4, where we dive into the fundamentals of budgeting. A budget serves as a financial roadmap, allocating funds to expenses such as rent, groceries, and entertainment, thus guiding you in effectively managing your hard-earned cash. Making a budget helps you avoid overspending, save money, and reach your financial goals. Think of it as a tool that puts you in charge of your money instead of letting your money control you.

Budgeting can be approached in two primary ways: the traditional, hands-on method or the modern, tech-friendly approach using budgeting software.

The classic, pen-and-paper method involves gathering your financial statements, bills, and a trusty notebook. Start by listing your income sources, including your job or any side hustles. Then, document your fixed expenses—those regular bills that remain constant, such as rent, utilities, and loan payments. Next, account for variable expenses—the ones that fluctuate, like groceries, dining out, and entertainment. Finally, subtract your total expenses from your income to get a clear snapshot of your financial situation.

But, in today's tech world, budgeting software has become a game-changer. Platforms like Mint, YNAB (You Need A Budget), and Every Dollar automate much of the budgeting process. They link to your bank accounts, sort your spending into categories, and show your money situation in easy-to-understand charts. They also offer features like goal tracking, debt payoff calculators, and spending breakdowns, giving you the full picture of your money story.

Whether you're scribbling on paper or tapping on a phone screen, a budget is essential for a few reasons.

First, it brings clarity to your financial situation. By outlining your income and expenses, a budget reveals where your money is going and how much is coming in. It can ensure that you have enough money to stretch until the next payday. This knowledge helps you make smart choices about your spending.

Second, a budget is like a financial GPS. It navigates you through the maze of expenses, preventing wrong turns that could lead to overspending or, worse, debt. It's your financial guardian, keeping you on track toward your financial goals.

A budget also helps you stay disciplined. Assigning every dollar a purpose stops you from making impulsive money moves and encourages you to manage your finances thoughtfully. When your goal is to pay off debt and build your savings, a budget helps you set and reach these goals. It turns your wishes into real, doable targets. It's acting as a guide to financial success.

SAMPLE OF A BUDGET

INCOME		
Paycheck 1		$ 2,000.00
Paycheck 2		$ 2,000.00
Total Income		**$ 4,000.00**
EXPENSES		
Mortgage or Rent	$,1200.00	
Utilities –gas, electric, etc	$ 300.00	
Car Payment	$ 400.00	
Car Insurance	$ 130.00	
Cell Bill	$ 100.00	
Internet Bill	$ 90.00	
Groceries	$ 300.00	
Gas for car	$ 250.00	
Cable TV	$ 100.00	
Gym membership	$ 100.00	
Student Loan	$ 300.00	
Credit Card Payment	$ 100.00	
Pet insurance fee	$ 125.00	
Restaurant –eating out	$ 250.00	
Music subscription	$ 10.99	
Netflix subscription	$ 20.00	
Apple iCloud storage	$ 9.99	
Delivery app subscription	$ 9.99	
Amazon Prime subscription	$ 14.99	
Xbox game pass subscription	$ 10.99	
Total Expenses	**$3,821.95**	
Income – Expenses		**$ 178.05**

In the sample, you can see that there is not much money left over. To expedite debt repayment, prioritize trimming non-essential expenses from your budget. Evaluate discretionary spending on items like streaming services, unused memberships, or excessive dining out. You could also look for a cheaper place to live or get a roommate. Any extra money can then be put toward your debt. This approach empowers you to regain control, turning small adjustments into impactful strides toward financial freedom.

CHAPTER 5

CUT BACK ON EXPENSES

Now that you've pinpointed your debts and crafted a budget, it's time to explore ways to cut back or eliminate expenses. While it may initially feel challenging, consider these measures as temporary sacrifices on your journey to financial stability. Here are some practical tips to help you reduce spending:

CUT OUT SUBSCRIPTION SERVICES

Cancel your magazine or newspaper subscriptions and read content online instead. Nowadays, many companies in the US are promoting subscription services, which can regularly take a chunk of your money. Combat this by assessing your subscriptions, canceling unnecessary ones, and negotiating better deals. Trim these expenses to bolster your savings and gain control over your finances. For example, choosing a one-time purchase of Microsoft Office is often more economical than committing to a yearly subscription. Once you buy the product, you own it, avoiding recurring payments. Other subscription examples include Xbox Live, Netflix, Amazon Prime, Spotify, Hulu, Disney +, and Dollar Shave Club. Assess what you really need and cancel the rest.

CUT BACK ON FOOD & DRINKS

1. Eliminate take-out, fast food, and food deliveries.

2. Host potluck-style gatherings with friends instead of dining out.

3. Share restaurant entrées, opt for water, and skip alcohol, coffee, or dessert.

4. Cook meals at home by finding recipes for your favorite dishes online.

5. Plan a weekly menu to avoid impulse purchases from restaurants/fast food places.

6. Shop at wholesale stores for cost-effective groceries.

7. Pack lunch for work to save on daily expenses.

8. Avoid buying snacks from vending machines; pack your own.

9. Minimize purchases from coffee stands; make drinks at home.

CUT BACK ON GROOMING & BEAUTY

1. Haircuts at Home: Invest in quality hair-cutting scissors and clippers to trim your hair at home. Watch tutorials on YouTube for step-by-step guidance for various styles.

2. DIY Hair Coloring: Skip the salon and try coloring your hair at home using store-bought kits.

3. Home Manicures/Pedicures: Save on salon visits by doing your own manicures and pedicures. Basic nail care tools and a variety of nail polish colors can be purchased inexpensively. You also risk getting nail fungus from a salon that re-uses files.

4. Choosing store-bought skincare products over expensive MLM (Multi-Level Marketing) options or celebrity-endorsed cosmetics can save you significant money. Store-bought skincare brands offer a wide range of affordable and effective options, often with similar or even superior ingredients compared to pricier alternatives.

5. Minimal Makeup Approach: Adopt a more natural look and minimize the use of expensive cosmetics. Focus on enhancing your features with fewer products, reducing the need for frequent restocking.

6. Getting fake eyelashes from a salon poses potential dangers, including allergic reactions, infections, and

damage to natural lashes. To save money and minimize risks, opting for mascara or embracing a natural look can be safer alternatives. Embracing natural beauty not only saves money but also eliminates the risks associated with salon procedures, promoting eye health and well-being.

7. Saving money on waxing can be achieved by using a store-bought waxing kit at home instead of going to a salon. Home waxing kits are cost-effective and convenient, offering similar hair removal results at a fraction of salon prices. By mastering the technique and following instructions carefully, individuals can achieve smooth, hair-free skin without the need for professional salon services.

8. Buy in Bulk: Purchase grooming essentials in larger quantities to take advantage of bulk discounts. This is especially beneficial for items like razors, shaving cream, and skincare products.

CUT BACK ON TRANSPORTATION COSTS

1. Downsize to a more fuel-efficient vehicle.

2. Consider swapping an expensive car for a more affordable option.

3. Explore alternatives like public transportation, carpooling, or biking.

4. Save on gas by combining errands into one trip.

5. Look for cheaper gas at wholesale stores or stores with rewards programs.

6. Avoid buying premium gas; use regular unleaded.

7. Limit joyrides and ask for gas contributions if giving rides.

8. Wash your car at home instead of using a car wash.

9. Raise your insurance deductible to reduce monthly rates.

10. Obtain insurance quotes annually for competitive rates.

CUT OUT OTHER UNNECESSARY EXPENSES

1. Cancel underutilized gym memberships and exercise at home.

2. Skip frequent dry cleaning; wear washer-friendly clothes.

3. Eliminate expensive habits like smoking to save money.

4. Reevaluate expensive hobbies; consider more frugal alternatives.

By adopting these strategies, you can make meaningful changes to your spending habits and work toward financial freedom.

CHAPTER 6

CREDIT REPORT AND CREDIT SCORE

A **credit report** is a comprehensive record of your credit history, encompassing credit cards, loans, and payment records with lenders, as well as any public records such as bankruptcies or tax liens. Similar to a report card reflecting your academic performance, a credit report shows how responsible you've been with your financial obligations.

A **credit score** is a numerical representation of your creditworthiness. Your credit score, similar to a grade on a report card, condenses the credit report information into a numerical value, ranging from 300 to 850. Just as a good grade reflects strong academic performance, a higher credit score indicates responsible financial behavior. Your credit score is crucial for securing future credit, loans, obtaining lower insurance, or even renting an apartment. Lenders use this score to assess your financial responsibility and determine the risk of lending to you. A higher credit score opens doors to better interest rates and more favorable terms, while a lower score may limit your financial opportunities.

Excellent:	750 & above
Good:	700 – 749
Fair:	650 – 699
Poor:	550 – 649
Bad:	550 & Below

What Are the 5 Factors That Affect Your Credit Score?

- Your payment history (35 percent)
- Amounts owed (30 percent)
- Length of your credit history (15 percent)
- Your credit mix (10 percent)
- Any new credit (10 percent)

Your credit score essentially reflects your debt management skills. Debt can be divided into two main categories: installment and revolving. Installment debt involves borrowing a fixed amount and repaying it in fixed, regular installments over a set period, like a car loan, student loan, or mortgage. On the other hand, revolving debt doesn't have a fixed end date, and you can borrow, repay, and borrow again up to a credit limit, like credit cards or a home equity line of credit.

It's essential to regularly check your credit report to verify accuracy, detect potential identity theft, and maintain a positive financial reputation. Errors such as incorrect account details or fraudulent activities can negatively impact your credit score. You can access a free credit report annually from each major credit bureau through AnnualCreditReport.com. The three nationwide consumer reporting companies include Equifax, TransUnion, and Experian. If you find any discrepancies within your credit report, you will want to contact these agencies to get them corrected.

You will also want to monitor and maintain your credit score. A high credit score is important for favorable loan terms, lower interest rates, and financial opportunities. Checking it annually helps ensure accuracy, detect errors, and maintain financial health, empowering you to make informed decisions and secure better financial prospects.

CHAPTER 7

CREDIT CARDS

C redit cards offer convenience and benefits, allowing users to build credit, earn rewards, and manage expenses. Its ease of obtainment allows individuals to establish a credit history. Making timely payments and maintaining a low credit utilization ratio contribute positively to one's credit score, fostering financial stability and enabling future opportunities, such as securing loans or renting an apartment. Responsible credit card usage can pave the way for a solid credit foundation.

However, misuse can lead to financial pitfalls. Relying on credit cards can diminish the emotional connection to spending, as it lacks the tangible nature of using cash. When using plastic, it's easier to overspend, as the immediate impact on one's wallet is not felt. Failure to pay off credit card balances can result in high-interest charges, accumulating debt, and negatively impacting credit scores. A missed payment can trigger fees and increased interest rates. Continuous debt accumulation may lead to a cycle of financial stress.

Imagine buying a $1,000 smartphone using a credit card with a 15% interest rate. If you only make minimum payments, interest becomes a relentless companion, accumulating rapidly. In this scenario, if you only paid the minimum balance each month at a 3% balance of your credit card, it will take you 83 months (nearly 7 years) to pay it off, and you will have paid an additional $507.99 in interest, $1,507.99 total ($1,000 + $507.99)

Example – If you only paid minimum payment at a **15% APR** credit card rate

Item	Price	Interest	Total	Months to Pay Off
Smartphone	$1,000	$507.99	$1,507.99	83

Another example is letting your credit card debt accumulate as lenders increase your credit limit. If you continuously allow it to grow and only make minimum monthly payments, you will be quite surprised at how quickly the debt total adds up. And if you miss a payment, the lender can quickly raise your interest rate.

Example – If you only paid minimum payment at a **20% APR** credit card rate

Item Payment	Amount to Pay Off	Minimum to Lender	Total Years	Total Interest Paid
CC Balance	$7,177.03	$199.12	19	$17,735

If you want to see how much money you're wasting on credit card interest, then look at the monthly statement to see the amount of interest charged on your purchases. In the scenario described, you're charged approximately $127 for holding a balance of $7,177.03 on your monthly statement. Then, take a look at your year-end statement to see the total interest you've been charged, for example, $1,754.66! Think of all those wealthy executives at the credit card companies who are living the high life...at your expense. That should make you angry and motivated to pay off your credit cards and vow to adopt a more frugal lifestyle to avoid getting yourself back into this kind of unnecessary debt.

Regularly monitoring expenses, creating a budget, and avoiding unnecessary debt can help maintain financial stability and a positive credit history. Responsible credit card usage involves paying balances in full and on time. When used wisely, they can be valuable tools, but when mishandled, they may lead to unexpected challenges.

CHAPTER 8

LOANS

Loans are a common financial tool for Americans, serving various needs. Auto loans help with vehicle purchases, student loans fund education, mortgages enable home ownership, and personal loans offer flexibility. A good credit score is pivotal in this financial process, influencing the interest rate on loans. A high credit score opens doors to more affordable loans. On the flip side, a poor credit score can be a financial hurdle, leading to higher interest rates and less favorable loan terms. Let's look at a few common loans: car loans, student loans, and home loans.

CAR LOANS

America is a car-driven society, and it is considered the second biggest purchase after a house. And they can get expensive rather quickly. Taking out a loan lets you own a car right away, but it's important to balance your car desires with smart financial choices. If you overspend on a car, it could lead to more debt and ongoing expenses, impacting your overall budget. It's like finding the right match between the car you want and what makes sense for your wallet, considering not just the loan payments but also other costs like insurance, maintenance, and fuel. So, when considering a car purchase, it's wise to consider both your dreams and your financial reality.

A frugal person approaches car ownership thoughtfully. Instead of taking on a large car loan, they might opt for a used vehicle. They understand depreciation and know that once you drive a new car off the lot, its value drops significantly. It's like losing money as soon as you take ownership, emphasizing the financial impact of financing a new vehicle. A frugal person will prefer driving an older car, allowing them to save money to purchase a car with cash instead of taking on debt.

STUDENT LOANS

Student loans come with both advantages and disadvantages. On the positive side, they provide financial support for students to attend college, making higher education accessible to a broader population. This access, however, comes with a hefty price tag. The cost of student loans can accumulate quickly, leading to substantial debt for graduates. One significant drawback is that not all students who take out loans end up completing their degree, leaving them with the burden of debt without the anticipated career benefits of a college education.

For those attending college in another state, out-of-state tuition adds an extra layer of financial strain. Out-of-state students typically face higher tuition costs than in-state counterparts, making their education significantly more expensive. This financial hurdle can lead to increased student loan debt and longer repayment periods. While pursuing education away from home can offer valuable experiences and opportunities, the financial implications must be carefully considered.

A frugal person uses smart strategies to handle student loans. Some skip college, opting for other paths like job training. Others work part-time while studying, earning money to cover some costs and reducing the need for loans. Some might choose to attend a community college for the first two years before transferring to a more affordable four-year school. This way, they save on tuition while still getting a degree.

HOME LOANS

Many Americans aspire to own a home, viewing it as a symbol of financial success. However, they often underestimate the complete financial picture. Homeownership comes with significant costs and responsibilities. Beyond the mortgage, additional expenses like insurance, property taxes, and maintenance can quickly add up. Homeowners also bear the burden of unforeseen repairs, from leaky toilets to malfunctioning furnaces, putting the responsibility on them versus calling a landlord to fix these issues.

In reality, a home loan requires a significant financial commitment, and neglecting the full scope of costs can lead to substantial debt.

Prospective homebuyers must diligently research, consider all expenses, and prepare for the financial responsibilities that accompany homeownership. It's important to understand that a considerable portion of payments will cover interest over the loan's duration. This emphasizes the necessity of evaluating the actual loan cost and grasping the financial commitment involved.

A frugal individual adopts a strategic approach to home loans by opting for a smaller loan amount. This might involve saving diligently for a larger down payment or choosing a more affordable property. Additionally, frugal thinkers might explore alternatives like renting or selecting a shorter loan term, such as a 15-year mortgage.

In summary, a frugal person would handle loans differently than an average person would. By prioritizing financial stability, frugal people avoid unnecessary or costly loans. These measures reflect a prudent financial mindset to ensure that they have a more secure financial future.

LOANS TO AVOID

Payday loans, title loans, and high-interest personal loans are examples of bad debt loans. These loans often come with exorbitant interest rates, hidden fees, and unfavorable terms, making them financially burdensome for borrowers. It's advisable to explore more reasonable and sustainable borrowing options to avoid the pitfalls associated with these types of loans.

CHAPTER 9

INTEREST RATES

Compound interest is a powerful financial concept that influences both investments and debts. When you invest money, compound interest allows your earnings to grow exponentially. Unlike simple interest, which applies only to the initial investment, compound interest accumulates on both your principal amount (how much you first invested) and the interest you've already earned. This creates a snowball effect, accelerating your returns over time. However, compounding interest isn't always favorable. When applied to high-interest debts like credit cards, it can significantly increase what you owe.

Here's an example of how compound interest works when investing $10,000 with a 10% annual interest rate:

By Year	Amount	Compound Interest	Note
1	$10,000	$11,000	$10,000 + $1,000 (10%)
2	$11,000	$12,100	$11,000 + $1,100 (10%)
3	$12,100	$13,310	$12,100 + $1,210 (10%)
4	$13,310	$14,641	$13,310 + $1,331 (10%)
5	$14,641	$16,105.10	$14,641 + $1,464.10 (10%)

After one year, your account grows to $11,000, including the $1,000 interest earned. In the fifth year, you earn interest on both the original $10,000 and the interest from the previous years, resulting in $16,105.10. This compounding effect continues, leading to exponential growth.

On the downside, when compounding interest is associated with debts, such as credit cards, it becomes a challenge to pay down balances. Most credit cards compound interest daily. This means that the interest you owe is added to your balance. If you have a credit card with a $5,000 balance and a 17% interest rate, making minimum payments of $100 monthly, it will take 86 months to pay off (a little over 7 years)!

Example – If you only paid minimum payment at a 17% APR credit card rate:

Item	Amount to Pay Off	Minimum Payment to Lender	Total Months	Interest Paid	Total Paid
CC Balance	$5,000	$100.00	86	$3,576.00	$8,576.00

In this scenario, you'd pay $8,576 total ($5,000 + $3,576 interest). Understanding compound interest is vital because it affects both savings and debts. It can significantly grow investments over time. It can also amplify credit card debt, leading to increased financial burden, or extend the time required to pay off payday loans. Therefore, it is vital to be aware of its impact to make informed financial decisions and avoid the pitfalls of accumulating high-interest debt.

Getting into debt can feel like an easy way to have what you want immediately, but it comes with a high price – interest. This makes debt a constant uphill battle.

CHAPTER 10

INSURANCE

W hile having an emergency fund is beneficial, some emergencies are too rare and costly to prepare for, especially during catastrophes. Securing insurance before you need it is essential for managing risks and avoiding financial ruin from traumatic events.

Insurance serves several important purposes:

1. Helps replace the cost of a new cellphone if your phone gets lost, damaged, or stolen.

2. Enables you to drive a vehicle by covering the high healthcare and legal expenses related to accidents and injuries.

3. Helps maintain your lifestyle if you face a disability or a critical illness.

4. Covers healthcare expenses, including prescription drugs, dental and vision care.

5. Allows you to own a home, as mortgage lenders require protection for your home.

6. Provides financial support for your family in case of your death.

You want to insure against what would be a huge financial loss for you or your dependents. When you buy insurance, you transfer potential loss costs to the insurance company in exchange for a premium. A **premium** is the amount of money you pay, usually on a monthly or yearly basis, for your coverage. Every company has a different way of analyzing how much of a risk you are. Your credit score can affect the premium – a higher score usually means a lower premium, highlighting the importance of maintaining good credit for affordable insurance.

CELLPHONE INSURANCE

Is cellphone insurance worth the money? For the majority of people, it is, especially with the cost of the latest smartphone averaging at $1,000. The insurance can help you avoid paying the full price of a replacement if your phone breaks, gets lost, or is stolen.

CAR INSURANCE

Once you get a car loan, you need insurance. The agent calculates your premium. Drivers with poor credit will pay a lot more for full coverage than those with good credit. If you file a claim after an accident, you pay a deductible before the insurance helps. A **deductible** is the amount you pay out of pocket for covered expenses before your insurance kicks in. For example, if your car needs $2,000 in repairs and you have a $500 deductible, you pay the first $500, and then the insurance covers the remaining $1,500.

HEALTH INSURANCE

Health insurance is necessary because it helps cover medical expenses, ensuring you don't face massive bills during unexpected illnesses or accidents. It allows you to access necessary healthcare without worrying about high costs, providing financial protection and peace of mind. Having health insurance ensures you can receive timely and appropriate medical care without the burden of substantial out-of-pocket expenses.

DISABILITY INSURANCE

In addition to health insurance, disability insurance is equally important. It provides financial protection if you are unable to work due to illness or injury, replacing a portion of your income to help cover essential living expenses. Disability insurance acts as a safety net, ensuring you have financial support during challenging times when your ability to work is compromised.

HOMEOWNER INSURANCE

In case of unexpected events like fires, natural disasters, or theft, homeowner insurance provides financial coverage. It not only helps repair or rebuild your home but also replaces or reimburses you for damaged or stolen possessions. Having homeowner insurance ensures that you don't bear the full financial burden of unexpected incidents, providing peace of mind and safeguarding your investment in your home.

RENTER'S INSURANCE

For those who rent, renter's insurance is equally important. While your landlord's insurance covers the structure, it doesn't protect your personal belongings. Renter's insurance steps in to safeguard your possessions, offering coverage for items damaged or stolen in events like fire or theft. Renter's insurance is a cost-effective way to protect your belongings, ensuring you don't face financial strain in the aftermath of unexpected incidents. Whether you own or rent, having the right insurance provides a safety net for your financial well-being.

LIFE INSURANCE

Life insurance is a financial safety net for your loved ones. In the event of your passing, it provides a lump sum payment, offering financial support to cover funeral expenses, outstanding debts, and living costs. This ensures that your family doesn't face financial strain during a challenging time. Life insurance is a responsible way to plan for the future, offering peace of mind and security for those you care about.

Term life insurance provides coverage for a specific period, such as 10, 20, or 30 years, offering a death benefit if you pass away during that term. It's generally more affordable because it doesn't accumulate cash value.

On the other hand, whole life insurance covers you for your entire life and includes a cash value component that grows over time. Whole life insurance can be expensive, and for many people, it may not be the most cost-effective option. The premiums are higher compared to term life insurance, making it less budget-friendly. Additionally, agents earn commissions for selling whole life policies, potentially influencing their recommendations. For those seeking affordable coverage with flexibility, term life insurance is often a more suitable choice, providing adequate protection without the added costs and complexities of whole life insurance.

Understanding insurance and making informed choices is vital to safeguard against unforeseen financial burdens. The price of insurance isn't cheap, but it's relatively small in comparison to the potential loss from a financial catastrophe. The problem lies in the unpredictability of when or what unfortunate events may befall you.

CHAPTER 11

JOBS AND SIDE HUSTLES

The aftermath of COVID-19 showed us that job security isn't guaranteed, and it's crucial to be prepared. If you lose your job, the first step is understanding your finances by creating a budget. Look for new job opportunities, consider different career paths, or take on temporary roles to keep income flowing. Even if you're still employed, it's wise to stay proactive. Keep your resume updated, explore career advancement, and be aware of market trends. Networking within your industry is essential for future opportunities.

Downsizing might be necessary whether you've lost your job or not. This could mean selling assets, moving to a more affordable place, or cutting back on non-essential spending. You could also look at other ways to increase your income. This extra money can help tackle outstanding debts and build an emergency fund.

Here are some practical ideas to make extra income:

Increase Your Work Income

1. Work overtime hours at your current job.

2. Consider asking for a pay raise if you believe you deserve it.

3. Apply for higher-paying positions within your company if opportunities arise.

Part-Time Work Ideas

1. Deliver food or work at a fast-food restaurant.

2. Become a driver for services like Uber or Lyft.

3. Work part-time as a store clerk.

4. Offer dog-walking or pet-sitting services.

5. Babysit for families in your community.

6. Consider bartending or working as a barista.

7. Offer house cleaning or janitorial services part-time.

8. Run errands or do shopping for others.

9. If you have expertise, explore consulting or event planning.

10. Seasonal opportunities like fire-fighting or guiding tours can be available in certain regions.

Creative Ventures:

1. Sell paintings or handmade crafts, especially during holidays.

2. Offer baking services, such as making wedding cakes.

3. Utilize photography skills for events or offer video production services.

4. Create and monetize content on platforms like YouTube.

5. Use tech skills to build websites for clients.

6. Consider writing a book, but be aware of the associated work and costs.

These ideas showcase various ways to generate extra income based on skills, interests, and available opportunities. It's important to explore options that align with your strengths and preferences. But beware of MLMs; they often promise riches but can lead to financial loss.

MLMs, or multi-level marketing companies, often target groups like stay-at-home moms, promising them a chance to earn extra income from home. MLM involves individuals selling products or services and recruiting others to do the same. While the appeal of making money on the side is enticing, it's important to understand that these companies make grand promises of passive income that rarely materialize. In reality, statistics show that over 99% of people involved in MLMs do not make a substantial profit and end up losing money instead of earning.

Sample of just a few MLM companies include:

1. Rodan & Fields (skincare)

2. LuLaRoe (clothing)

3. Herbalife (nutrition)

4. Avon, Mary Kay, Younique (cosmetics)

5. Young Living (essential oils)

6. Amway (health and beauty)

7. Paparazzi (jewelry)

Note: While these companies use MLM structures, it's essential to approach them with caution due to the potential risks associated with such business models. A captivating example is the docuseries "LuLaRich" that is available to watch on Amazon Prime. "LuLaRich" delves into the world of LuLaRoe, an MLM company renowned for its dizzying leggings. Spanning four 45-minute episodes, the directors shed light on the company's darker aspects. Through testimonies from various individuals, the series unveils the intricate ways in which LuLaRoe engages with past, present, and prospective members, depicting it as more than just an ordinary MLM but rather verging on cult-like behavior.

MLMs gained popularity during the pandemic due to increased interest in remote work and flexible income opportunities. However, they often operate like pyramid schemes, where only a few at the top make significant profits while the majority struggle to see any returns. The risks in MLMs include high upfront costs, pressure to recruit, and reliance on recruitment for income. Thoroughly research any MLM and be cautious of promises that seem **too good to be true**.

In summary, the job market is unpredictable, so adaptability is key. Regularly review your career options, stay financially flexible, and focus on reducing debt. Creating an emergency fund is critical to handle unexpected expenses without relying on credit. Instead of venturing into MLMs, there are alternative side hustles that offer more reliable income. Driving for ride-share companies, delivering food, or freelancing are examples. These options allow for flexibility, immediate income, and a better understanding of the effort-to-reward ratio. It's essential to choose side hustles wisely, considering both short-term gains and long-term sustainability.

CHAPTER 12

DOWNSIZING

Now that you've identified your debts and established a budget, tackling them might seem daunting, but there's a way forward. To make a significant dent in your debt, consider a strategic plan involving expense reduction, additional income, and downsizing.

One effective approach is to evaluate items around your home that are seldom used but have value. Selling such items through platforms like Craigslist, Facebook Marketplace, or a yard sale can generate extra income.

Taking steps to declutter or part with a home can be emotionally tough, but it can lead to financial freedom and a more affordable lifestyle. Here's how to make it more manageable:

1. Focus on the Benefits: Remind yourself of the benefits of decluttering and downsizing, like paying off debts, reduced stress, and achieving your goal of financial freedom.

2. Prioritize Items: Keep what truly matters to you and consider letting go of non-essential things. Focus on what brings value to your life.

3. Donate or Sell: Consider donating items in good condition to charity or selling them to generate extra income. Letting go of items that no longer serve a purpose can be easier when you know they will benefit someone else or contribute to your financial goals.

4. Embrace Minimalism: Shift your mindset to value experiences over possessions. Embracing minimalism can make letting go of clutter easier as you focus on what truly matters. Start by taking small, manageable steps if you feel overwhelmed. Tackle one room or area at a time.

5. Letting Go: Practice letting go of items that no longer serve you, even if they hold sentimental value. Remember that memories are not tied to physical possessions, and letting go can create space for new experiences and opportunities.

6. Roommate: Consider the option of getting a roommate to generate extra income. Renting out a room in your home can help offset expenses and provide additional financial stability. Make sure to screen potential roommates carefully to ensure compatibility and safety.

7. Digital Decluttering: Clear out digital clutter by organizing and deleting unnecessary files, emails, and digital

documents. Streamline your digital life to reduce stress and improve productivity.

The process is unique to each person, so take the time you need. Whether it's a few items or a larger-scale downsizing effort, these steps contribute to your overall strategy for shedding debt. It's a proactive and practical way to free up funds, accelerate debt repayment, and move closer to financial freedom.

A frugal person approaching downsizing adopts a practical mindset, prioritizing financial efficiency. They look at what they really need and what's important to them. They prefer experiences over having lots of stuff. They sell or give away things they don't use much, choosing a simpler way of living.

DOWNSIZING A HOME

If you can't afford the home you're living in, seeking a more affordable living situation may be a necessary step. This could also be a viable option when individuals or families find themselves with an empty nest. With grown children no longer residing in the family home, the space may be underutilized and financially burdensome. In such cases, downsizing to a smaller, more affordable home can offer numerous benefits, including reduced living expenses, lower mortgage payments, decreased property taxes, and simplified maintenance requirements. Moreover, downsizing can free up equity in the home, providing much-needed funds to pay off debt, bolster savings, or invest for retirement.

Preparing a home for sale is a vital step in the process, and there are several key steps to consider:

1. Declutter and Depersonalize: Begin by decluttering the home and removing personal items such as family photos, memorabilia, and excessive decorations. Depersonalizing the space allows potential buyers to envision themselves living in the home.

2. Deep Clean: Ensure the home is thoroughly cleaned, including scrubbing floors, walls, and surfaces and addressing any odors. Consider hiring professional cleaners for a more thorough job.

3. Make Repairs: Address any necessary repairs or maintenance issues throughout the home. This may include fixing leaky faucets, repairing damaged walls or flooring, replacing broken fixtures, and ensuring all systems (plumbing, HVAC, electrical) are in working order.

4. Enhance Curb Appeal: First impressions matter, so invest time and effort in enhancing the home's curb appeal. This may involve landscaping, painting the exterior, repairing or replacing the roof, updating the front door, and ensuring pathways and driveways are clean and well-maintained.

5. Neutralize Décor: Paint walls in neutral colors to appeal to a broader range of buyers. Neutral décor creates a blank

canvas that allows potential buyers to envision their own style and preferences in the space.

6. Maximize Space: Arrange furniture to maximize space and flow throughout the home. Remove bulky or excess furniture to create a more spacious feel, especially in smaller rooms.

7. Highlight Features: Showcase the home's best features and amenities. This may include staging rooms to highlight functionality and versatility, emphasizing natural light and views, and accentuating architectural details.

8. Invest in Staging: Consider hiring a professional stager to optimize the presentation of the home. Staging can help highlight the property's strengths, create an inviting atmosphere, and increase its appeal to potential buyers.

9. Professional Photography: Invest in professional photography to showcase the home in its best light. High-quality photos are essential for online listings and marketing materials, attracting more potential buyers to view the property.

10. Price Competitively: Work with a real estate agent to determine the optimal listing price for the home based on market conditions, comparable sales, and the property's condition and features. Competitive pricing can attract more buyers and increase the likelihood of a quicker sale.

By taking these steps to prepare the home for sale, individuals can enhance its appeal, attract more potential buyers, and ultimately increase the likelihood of a successful sale. Downsizing to a more affordable home can offer financial relief and a fresh start, allowing individuals to regain control of their finances and move toward a more secure financial future.

CHAPTER 13

SAVE AROUND THE HOUSE

It's essential not only to cut back on expenses but also to find ways to save money around your home. By being proactive and implementing simple changes, you can significantly reduce your monthly spending and increase your savings.

Here are 20 simple ways to save money around your home:

1. Consider using less toothpaste; you'll be surprised how much longer these products last.

2. Consider using less shampoo.

3. Consider using less laundry detergent.

4. Wash clothes in cold water to save on energy costs.

5. Hang clothes to dry instead of using the dryer.

6. Consider using less dishwasher detergent and allow your dishes to air dry. Opt for handwashing dishes for a few items instead of running the dishwasher.

7. Use a hand rag instead of paper towels.

8. Invest in real dishes instead of buying disposable plates; it's not only more eco-friendly but also cost-effective.

9. Cook meals at home instead of dining out.

10. Bulk Buying: Purchase non-perishable items in bulk to benefit from lower unit prices.

11. DIY Cleaning Products: Make your own cleaning solutions using household items like vinegar and baking soda.

12. Cut your dish scrubber in half to use when you hand wash dishes.

13. Reusable Containers: Invest in reusable containers for food storage instead of using disposable bags or wraps.

14. Second-Hand Furniture: Consider buying used furniture or repurposing existing items to save on home decor costs.

15. Clothing Swaps: Organize clothing swaps with friends or family to refresh your wardrobe without spending money.

16. DIY Home Decor: Get creative and make your own home decor items, from wall art to throw pillows.

17. Thrift Shopping: Explore thrift stores for clothing, furniture, and household items at budget-friendly prices.

18. Gardening: Grow your own herbs and vegetables to save on grocery bills and enjoy fresh produce.

19. Conduct regular maintenance on appliances to ensure they operate efficiently and last longer.

20. Repair Instead of Replace: Opt for repairs over replacements to minimize expenses whenever items break down.

Implementing these simple tips can help you save money and cultivate a more frugal and sustainable lifestyle.

CHAPTER 14

SAVE ON UTILITIES

Managing your home's energy use plays a big role in your budget. These changes not only help the environment but also mean more cash in your pocket for things you really need or to help pay down debt. Here are practical tips to cut costs.

ELECTRICITY USE

Small steps can add up to big reductions in your electricity use— and your utility bill.

1. Using auto shut-off devices for appliances like coffee pots, crock pots, or curling irons is beneficial for both saving on electricity bills and preventing fire hazards. These devices automatically turn off the appliance after a set period.

2. Turn things off. Flip the light switch when you leave a room (even if it's just for a few minutes). You should also make sure your TV, cable box, digital recorder, video game console, charges for cell phones and tablets, computers, printers,

and other devices are switched off when you're not actively using them. They use small amounts of energy even when they're not charging.

3. Computers can also be set to sleep or hibernate mode, which uses much less power than when they're on and active; program yours to do this automatically after 10 to 15 minutes of inactivity. And skip the screen savers; they're not necessary to protect modern monitors. Opt for laptops over desktop computers when purchasing new ones, as they generally consume less power. You can also use your laptop for hours without having it plugged in to save on electricity.

4. When you're not using electronic devices, they may still continue drawing electricity, also known as vampire energy or phantom power. Although on their own, each device only uses a modest amount of power, the collective impact of all your home's devices can constitute a substantial portion of your electricity use. Plug items you use regularly into a power strip so you can easily switch them all off at once. Unplug devices such as hair dryers, electric shavers, and smart kitchen appliances as well.

5. Switch to energy-efficient bulbs such as LEDs. Consider motion-sensor outdoor lights and switch to dusk-till-dawn LED bulbs.

6. Install dimmer switches. A light dimmer is a device that controls the brightness of a light fixture. It can help you save energy because it reduces the flow of electricity to the bulb, so the light operates with less power. That means you save money on your electric bill — and your light bulbs last longer, too.

While it may not be practical to unplug all appliances regularly—such as your refrigerator, which requires constant operation—combating vampire energy is achievable for most other electronic devices. For example, if you need your WIFI router plugged in to check your home alarm system or cameras, or if your DVR needs to stay on to record shows, consider plugging them into separate outlets, away from the power strip. However, there are a handful of practical steps you can take to combat vampire energy and reduce your electricity costs.

HEATING AND COOLING

1. The clothes dryer is one of the largest energy users in the home. When using your dryer, you can reduce energy consumption by drying your clothes for five to ten minutes, and then taking them out to air dry. Use liquid fabric softener to prevent static issues with clothes.

2. Don't run the dishwasher when it's not full. If you have an older dishwasher, turn off the heat dry function and allow your dishes to air dry. You can gently shake the top

rack to get the excess water off. You can also save money by handwashing dishes in the sink or washing dishes in two giant bowls: one to wash and one to rinse.

3. Reduce hot water usage by taking shorter showers and fixing leaks promptly. Replace old showerheads with new low-flow designs to prevent excess hot water from going down the drain.

4. Lower the thermostat on your water heater and insulate it if possible. Use hot water wisely to conserve energy.

5. Use cold water to wash your laundry and save money versus using hot water. Cold water is better for your clothes, too, since it helps prevent shrinking, fading and wrinkling.

6. Regularly clean the lint filter after each use of the clothes dryer.

7. Regularly clean the coils behind the refrigerator. Your refrigerator coils are a magnet for dirt and dust, and the more that collects, the harder it has to run to keep your food cold. This should be done at least once a year.

8. Ceiling fans should rotate clockwise in winter to redistribute warm air and counterclockwise in summer for a cooling effect. Fans can help maintain comfortable

temperatures without relying on heating or cooling systems.

9. In colder climates, open blinds during the day to allow sunlight and close them at night for insulation. In warmer climates, cover your windows with window films or solar-type screens to keep the extra heat from coming into the home.

10. Set your thermostat lower when away or at night when sleeping. Take caution turning your heat down too low, especially during winter months, to avoid freezing pipes.

11. If you haven't done so already, it might be time to switch to a programmable or smart thermostat that can be set to adjust the temperature in your home at certain hours of the day. Smart thermostats enable you to maintain a comfortable temperature in your home and many of them can be operated remotely — even from your smartphone.

12. If you live in a cold climate, don't plug in your car all night. Use a cord with a timer instead.

13. You'll save more money on air conditioning bills the closer you keep your inside temperature to the outside temperature, so see if you can stand to set your thermostat at 78 instead of 72. It may take some getting used to, and you may have to shed some layers, but

you'll appreciate it when your energy bill goes down. Invest in a programmable thermostat and schedule it to increase to 80°F when no one is home during the day, and you'll save even more.

14. Dirty filters block airflow, making your air conditioner work harder to cool your home. Clogged filters also increase the chance that you'll end up needing air conditioner repair, so change your filter once a month during the hot summer to lower cooling bills and extend the life of your air conditioning system. Routine preventative maintenance on your A/C is the best way to avoid needing HVAC repairs.

15. Improve your insulation. When your heating and cooling system pumps air into your home, some of that air can escape through poorly insulated walls, floors and ceilings. That causes major energy waste and makes your home less comfortable. Attic insulation, air sealing and floor and crawl space insulation will keep your house warm in the winter and cool in the summer.

16. Seal up your house. After insulating your home, it's a good idea to find the other nooks and crannies where air may escape. Address heat escape points like gaps around doors and windows. Weatherstrip and use draft stoppers.

17. Ask about discounted rates. Some utility companies offer "time of use" plans, where your electricity rates are based on the time of day you consume electricity. You pay lower rates during off-peak hours, which vary by utility and region. Activities such as doing your laundry, running the dishwasher and charging your electric vehicle during off-peak hours — usually between 9 p.m. and 6 a.m. — can help you save.

18. When your old appliances are due for replacement, you can consider ENERGY STAR-rated appliances, as they can save you more money upfront and for years into the future.

PHONE, CABLE and INTERNET

1. Consider eliminating your landline and using your cell phone as the primary.

2. Opt for a family cell phone plan with the same brand of phones. This way, everyone can use the same cell charger.

3. Downgrade your phone, cable, or internet plan if you don't use them often. Save money by choosing a plan that better suits your needs.

4. Ditch cable TV and switch to streaming services using your internet connection. Cable TV subscriptions can be

expensive, and streaming services offer more flexibility and cost-effective alternatives. By canceling cable and relying on streaming platforms, you pay only for the content you want to watch, often at a fraction of the cost. You can use devices like Apple TV or Roku to access shows and movies. Make sure to have a reliable internet package for smooth streaming.

TRASH OUTPUT

1. Bring reusable bags to the grocery store.

2. Eat meals with real plates and silverware and avoid using paper/plastic products.

3. Use reusable water bottles and food storage containers.

4. Reduce the number of times you get take-out meals.

5. Buy in bulk to reduce packaging waste.

6. Start recycling and reusing as much as possible.

In our fast-paced lives, convenience-driven technologies aim to save time and effort, such as automatic vacuums or voice assistants like Alexa, but there's a hidden cost. As reliance on these devices grows, so does the burden on wallets and the environment. A frugal approach emphasizes energy-efficient habits over unnecessary gadgets, to help save money in the long run.

CHAPTER 15

SAVE ON GROCERIES

S aving on groceries is a practical and effective way to manage your budget. You can significantly reduce your grocery expenses by adopting strategic shopping habits, making conscious choices, and implementing smart planning. Here are several tips to help you save on groceries:

1. Minimize Food Waste: Consuming items from your pantry before restocking reduces waste and ensures that food doesn't sit unused on your shelves.

2. Create a Budget: Before heading to the store, establish a realistic budget for your groceries. Having a clear spending limit helps you avoid unnecessary purchases.

3. Make a List: Before heading to the grocery store, go through your pantry, cupboards, or fridge, and create a list of items

you need. Stick to this list to avoid impulse purchases, and refrain from shopping while hungry to stay within budget. Stay focused and compare prices. Planning ahead helps curb unnecessary spending and promotes smarter, more budget-conscious shopping.

4. Avoid Grocery Store Tricks: Stay vigilant against grocery store tricks, including end-of-aisle displays, in-aisle eye-level displays, and checkout temptations. Stick to your list to resist impulse buys.

5. Utilize Coupons and Discounts: Keep an eye out for coupons and discounts. Many stores offer loyalty programs, digital coupons, and discounts on specific items. Take advantage of these to maximize savings.

6. Join a Rewards Program: Many grocery stores offer rewards programs that provide discounts, cashback, or points for future purchases. Sign up for these programs to enjoy additional savings.

7. Buy Generic or Store Brands: Choose generic or store-brand products instead of name brands. These items often provide similar quality at a lower cost, contributing to substantial savings over time.

8. Compare Prices: Be mindful of unit prices when shopping. Larger packaging doesn't always mean a better deal.

Compare unit prices to determine the most cost-effective option.

9. Purchase in Bulk: Consider buying non-perishable items in bulk, especially those with a longer shelf life. This can reduce the cost per unit and minimize the frequency of shopping trips.

10. Limit Convenience Foods: Pre-packaged and convenience foods are often more expensive. For instance, opt for stick butter instead of butter in a plastic container, reducing both costs and environmental impact.

11. Save on Coffee: Choosing a regular coffee pot and filter over a Keurig machine can save money and reduce environmental impact. With a traditional coffee pot, you buy coffee grounds in bulk, which is more cost-effective than individual Keurig pods, reducing plastic waste in landfills.

12. Track Prices and Sales Cycles: Pay attention to price fluctuations and sales cycles for the items you regularly purchase. Stock up when prices are low, especially during sales, to stretch your budget further.

13. Create a Weekly Menu: Plan your meals ahead and post the menu on the fridge. This simple step minimizes spontaneous restaurant outings, encourages home-cooked meals, and contributes to both financial savings and a healthier lifestyle.

14. Cooking at home doesn't have to be complicated. Use simple ingredients and package leftovers for the next day or pack for lunch.

15. If hunting or fishing is allowed where you live, you can slash your grocery expenses. This not only provides you with fresh ingredients but also lowers your grocery costs, making you more self-reliant.

16. Canning foods like meat, salmon, or seasonal produce is a cost-effective way to preserve food and save money by eliminating the need for refrigeration. Canning also allows you to enjoy home-canned meals at a fraction of the cost of store-bought equivalents.

Combining these strategies can transform your grocery shopping experience into a budget-friendly and organized routine. Consistent planning, use of discounts and rewards, and a mindful approach to purchases will empower you to save money, reduce waste, and enjoy nutritious meals. Remember, a little practice and organization go a long way in alleviating stress and enhancing your overall financial well-being.

CHAPTER 16

SAVE ON GAS

C utting back on how much you drive is a smart move to save money and help the environment. With gas prices on the rise, using less gasoline is good for your wallet.

Here are 20 simple ways to save money on gasoline:

1. Drive Efficiently: Avoid rapid acceleration and braking, and maintain a steady speed.

2. Combine Trips: Plan your errands to minimize driving distance and time.

3. Don't sign up: It's okay to resist signing up your children in numerous activities to avoid constant driving, saving both time and money.

4. Use Public Transportation: Opt for buses, trains, or carpooling when possible.

5. Walk or Bike: Short trips can be done by walking or biking instead of driving.

6. Maintain Your Vehicle: Keep your car well-maintained with regular tune-ups, oil changes, and tire checks.

7. Check Tire Pressure: Properly inflated tires improve fuel efficiency.

8. Reduce Weight: Remove unnecessary items from your car to reduce weight and improve gas mileage.

9. Avoid Idling: Turn off your engine if you're parked for more than a minute.

10. Use Cruise Control: On highways, cruise control can help maintain a consistent speed and save fuel.

11. Drive Slower: High speeds increase fuel consumption, so stick to the speed limit.

12. Avoid Roof Racks: Remove roof racks when not in use to reduce aerodynamic drag.

13. Avoid Aggressive Driving: Rapid acceleration and braking waste fuel.

14. Choose Efficient Routes: Use GPS apps to find the most fuel-efficient routes.

15. Use Air Conditioning Wisely: Use AC sparingly, as it increases fuel consumption.

16. Shop Around for Gas: Compare prices at different gas stations and use loyalty programs for discounts.

17. Use Gas Apps: Use apps to find the cheapest gas stations along your route.

18. Consider Fuel-efficient Vehicles: If buying a new car, choose one with high fuel efficiency.

19. Avoid Rush Hour: Traffic congestion leads to stop-and-go driving, which wastes fuel.

20. Car Maintenance: Keep your car in top condition to ensure optimal fuel efficiency.

21. Consider Hybrid or Electric Vehicles: If feasible, switch to a hybrid or electric vehicle for significant long-term fuel savings.

Implementing these tips can help you save money on gasoline and reduce your overall fuel expenses. These simple changes can really bring down how much you spend on gas every month. So, not only do you keep more money in your pocket, but you're also doing your part for the planet.

CHAPTER 17

SAVE ON ENTERTAINMENT

I n a quest for frugality, finding ways to save on entertainment and recreational activities can significantly impact your budget. Here are practical tips to cut costs without sacrificing fun:

SAVE ON MOVIES:

1. Matinee and Discount Days: Opt for matinee showings or theaters with discount days to slash ticket prices.

2. Discount Theaters: Explore discount theaters for a more budget-friendly movie experience.

3. Stream at Home: Utilize streaming services like Netflix or Hulu for cost-effective home entertainment.

4. Rent Instead of Buying: Resist the urge to purchase new movies; instead, rent or borrow to save on costs. For new online movie releases, wait to rent versus purchasing them.

5. Utilize Kiosk Rentals: Rent DVD or Blu-ray movies through kiosks like Redbox.

6. Review Cable Expenses: Evaluate cable subscriptions, consider canceling premium channels, and negotiate promotional rates.

OTHER ENTERTAINMENT SAVINGS:

1. Free Music Sources: Utilize internet services like YouTube for music or tune in to the radio for cost-effective entertainment options.

2. Music Purchases: Avoid buying full albums; use platforms like iTunes to purchase the song and own it versus paying monthly for a music subscription.

3. Fitness: Cancel underused gym memberships or switch to a more affordable gym to save money. Regularly reassess your fitness needs and evaluate the cost-effectiveness of your current membership.

4. Game Nights: Embrace board games or card games for some family bonding, or invite friends to join in the board game fun.

5. Get-togethers at Home: Save money by hosting potluck dinners at home instead of dining out with friends. Rotate the hosting responsibilities to different friends' homes, allowing everyone to contribute with side dishes.

6. Staycations: Save money by choosing staycations over expensive vacations. Keep your leisure activities close to home to reduce travel and accommodation costs.

7. Library Card Benefits: Utilize library resources for free books, music, and movie rentals.

8. Explore Local Museums or Attractions: Visit local museums or nearby attractions such as zoos, inquire about resident discounts, and enjoy educational outings.

9. Outdoor Activities: Engage in outdoor activities like walking, hiking, biking, tennis, frisbee golf, camping, and fishing.

By adopting these frugal practices, you can find simple joy and budget-friendly activities without breaking the bank.

CHAPTER 18

PREVENTING IDENTITY THEFT

I n today's digital age, identity theft poses a significant threat, as fraudsters can exploit your sensitive data, potentially leading to financial ruin. Frequent data breaches make it critical to take proactive steps to prevent identity theft. This chapter outlines the methods identity thieves use, potential risks, and steps to safeguard your identity.

HOW THIEVES OBTAIN YOUR INFO:

1. Social Security Number (SSN): Avoid carrying your SSN card or birth certificate.

2. Mail Theft: Secure Your Mailbox. Shred sensitive documents and opt for online statements whenever possible.

3. Phishing: Avoid responding to unsolicited emails or texts requesting sensitive information.

4. Spoofing: Be cautious of official-looking emails and never disclose personal data. Verify requests for sensitive information through other means before responding.

5. Unsafe Internet Connections: Avoid Public Wi-Fi: Refrain from entering personal info on public Wi-Fi networks.

6. Weak Data Protection: Protect personal information even within your home.

7. Data Breaches: Be aware of news about companies experiencing data breaches.

WHAT CAN IDENTITY THIEVES DO?

Identity thieves can exploit your information in various ways, ranging from obtaining new IDs to making unauthorized purchases. Recognizing these potential actions is vital for effective prevention. Here is a list of steps that you can take to protect your personal data.

1. Freeze Your Credit: Freeze your credit with Equifax, Experian, and TransUnion to prevent new credit files from being opened.

2. Safeguard Your SSN: Guard your Social Security number, avoid carrying your card, and securely store or shred related paperwork.

3. Be Alert to Phishing and Spoofing: Verify the legitimacy of calls or emails by initiating contact through known entities.

4. Use Strong Passwords and Add an Authentication Step: Utilize a password manager for complex, unique passwords, and consider adding a two-factor authentication to your account.

5. Use Alerts: Sign up for alerts from financial institutions to receive notifications about transactions.

6. Watch Your Mailbox: Hold your mail when away, use lockable mailboxes, or sign up for Informed Delivery through USPS.

7. Shred, Shred, Shred: Shred credit card, bank, and investment statements, along with preapproved credit offers.

8. Use a Digital Wallet: Opt for digital wallets for online and in-store payments, ensuring encrypted transactions.

9. Protect Your Mobile Devices: Use passwords on electronic devices and prefer banking apps over mobile browsers.

10. Social Media Caution: Limit personal information on social media, use privacy settings, and be cautious about friend requests.

11. Stay Skeptical: Be wary of scams and offers that **seem too good to be true**.

12. Check Your Credit Reports Regularly: Access free credit reports to ensure accurate reporting and watch for signs of fraud.

10. Monitor Financial and Medical Statements: Read financial statements, recognize every transaction, and review medical statements to guard against fraud.

WHAT TO DO IF YOUR IDENTITY IS STOLEN:

1. Act Immediately: Check bank and credit card statements. Alert your bank. Create an FTC Identity Theft Report.

2. Credit Bureaus Alert: Report to credit bureaus. Place a fraud alert—dispute inaccurate information on your credit report.

3. Credit Freeze: Consider a credit freeze to prevent new accounts from being opened.

4. Debt Collector Alert: Notify the company involved. Dispute fraudulent debt. Cease debt collectors' contact.

ADDITIONAL RESOURCES:

Visit www.identitytheft.gov for comprehensive information.

Being proactive in safeguarding your information and understanding the steps to take if your identity is compromised is imperative for managing your finances. Stay informed, stay cautious, and take action promptly to mitigate the impact of identity theft.

CHAPTER 19

PREVENTING HOME OR CAR THEFT

Protecting your home and car is paramount due to the prevalence of theft, which can have serious consequences. Here are some practical tips and preventive measures to safeguard your home and car:

PREVENTING HOME THEFT

1. Reinforce Entry Points: Install a peephole or deadbolt on your front door. Keep doors locked, even when at home or away briefly.

2. Garage Security: Conceal your garage door opener in your car. Cover windows near doors to prevent visibility.

3. Dispose of Boxes Discreetly: Break down boxes of valuable items before disposal. Avoid advertising recent purchases (for example—new TV) to potential thieves.

4. Key Safety: Avoid hiding spare keys near the main entry. Invest in a keypad deadbolt for added security.

5. Lighting and Security: Use motion-sensor floodlights or dusk-to-dawn bulbs. When away, create the illusion of an occupied home with lamps on timers.

6. Additional Security Measures: Utilize adjustable door security bars. They can be propped up against the door handle or placed in the sliding door area. Consider investing in a home safe for valuables.

7. Deterrence Tactics: Display fake alarm signs and stickers. Install a fake camera near entrances. Develop connections with neighbors for enhanced vigilance.

8. Social Media Caution: Avoid sharing vacation plans on social media. Keep a low profile regarding your absence.

9. Car Keys: Keep your car keys and cell phone next to your bed at night. Use the car remote's panic button if needed.

10. Consider DIY alarm systems: You can install a Guardline Driveway Alarm (sold on Amazon) in your mailbox to alert you of anyone coming into your yard.

11. Low-Cost Alarm Systems: Consider using alarm systems like SimpliSafe, which allows you to purchase the equipment upfront and pay a reasonable monthly fee, offering flexibility without contracts. In contrast, avoid

companies that require hefty monthly payments and long-term contracts. Evaluate alarm system options carefully before committing.

12. Personal Safety Measures: Consider owning a dog for added security. If comfortable, invest in personal protection tools or weapons.

13. Travel Plans: Before traveling, inform family or neighbors about your plans and have someone check your home regularly. Opt for lamp timers to come on during evening hours and cancel any newspaper subscription or package deliveries while you're away. Delay social media posts until after your trip.

PREVENTING CAR THEFT

1. Key Management: Avoid hiding spare keys in or around your car.

2. Door Locks: Double-check to make sure that you close the windows and lock all the doors before leaving the car.

3. Conceal Valuables: Keep valuables out of sight in your vehicle. Consider tinting windows for added privacy.

4. Avoid Leaving Cars Running: Refrain from leaving your car running unattended. Install an auto-start system for remote ignition control.

5. Physical Anti-Theft Devices: Use steering wheel locks or car clubs. Invest in a tech-based auto recovery tool with GPS tracking.

6. VIN Etching: Etch your VIN on windows for identification. Avoid displaying your home address on car registrations.

7. Strategic Parking: Choose well-lit areas for parking. Park in areas with high pedestrian traffic. Try to avoid parking next to large vans or SUVs that give a thief privacy.

8. Holidays: During holiday shopping, find a parking space as close as you can to the store entrance and park under a light if it's dark outside. Conceal your packages in the trunk if you continue shopping, or better yet, take them home.

9. Stay Alert: Be vigilant for signs of car thieves. Report suspicious activities to the police.

WHAT TO DO IF YOUR CAR IS STOLEN

1. Avoid Confrontation: Do not confront car thieves; prioritize personal safety.

2. Stay Calm and Call the Police: Provide details like make, model, license plate, and color. You can put your license plate in your phone's Notes in case you forget.

3. Document and Share Information: Share vehicle details, photos, and the case number on social media.

4. Contact Insurance Company: Inform your insurance company immediately.

Implementing these tips and preventive measures can significantly reduce the risk of home and car theft. Prioritize your safety, stay vigilant, and take proactive steps to secure your property. Combining these strategies enhances overall security, providing peace of mind for you and your loved ones.

CHAPTER 20

PROTECT YOURSELF FROM SCAMS

Scammers employ diverse tactics, from fake real estate seminars to online phishing, preying on unsuspecting individuals. Awareness is key to avoiding scams. As the saying goes, "If it sounds too good to be true, it probably is." Here's an in-depth look at prevalent scams and how to safeguard yourself.

WAYS SCAMMERS EXTRACT INFORMATION:

Phishing and Spoofing: These cyber threats aim to compromise your data. Phishing involves tricking you into divulging sensitive information, while spoofing employs malware to infiltrate your computer or network. Scammers often impersonate businesses via calls or fake emails. Be cautious, verify sender email addresses, and avoid clicking on suspicious attachments.

A CLOSER LOOK AT SOME VARIOUS SCAMS:

1. Phishing Emails: Scammers use deceptive emails, often posing as reputable entities, to trick individuals into revealing personal information.

2. Real Estate Rental Scams: Scammers create fake rental listings, deceiving both property owners and potential tenants. Travelers may pay for non-existent or unavailable properties. Always use reputable platforms, verify listings, and communicate directly with property owners.

3. Fake Orders or Cancellations: Beware of emails claiming orders have been made or canceled on your behalf if you didn't make them, especially if they urge you to click on links. Instead, visit the official website to check the status of any orders. Avoid potential malware threats and never disclose personal information through suspicious emails.

4. Romance Scams: Perpetrators create fake online profiles to establish romantic relationships and later request money for various reasons.

5. IRS Impersonation: Scammers pose as IRS agents, making threatening calls to coerce individuals into making immediate payments or divulging sensitive information.

6. Lottery or Prize Scams: Victims receive notifications of winning a lottery or prize, but to claim it, they must pay fees or provide personal details.

7. Get Rich Quick in Real Estate: Avoid seminars promising quick riches through real estate investment. Often, these events exploit attendees by selling books or future seminars. Real estate success requires hard work and careful consideration, not shortcuts or get-rich-quick schemes.

8. Social Media Impersonation: Scammers create fake profiles of celebrities or friends to solicit money or personal information from unsuspecting individuals.

9. Investment Fraud: Fraudulent investment schemes promise guaranteed high returns, pressuring victims to invest without proper information. When investing, thoroughly research and only invest in what you understand to mitigate risks. Exercise caution with cryptocurrency investments due to their volatile nature and susceptibility to scams. Many individuals have fallen victim to crypto-related frauds, emphasizing the importance of informed and careful investment decisions in the digital asset space.

10. Multi-Level Marketing (MLM) Schemes: Many MLM businesses fail, relying on individuals to market products

to friends and family. Beware of high-pressure tactics and unrealistic promises. Research complaints before joining any MLM venture.

11. Modeling Schools: Modeling scams exploit individuals' dreams of a glamorous career. Avoid paying for fake training or photo sessions, and be skeptical of tryouts held in malls or hotels.

HOW TO PROTECT YOURSELF FROM SCAMS:

1. Shred Personal Documents: Safeguard sensitive information by shredding documents and receipts containing personal details.

2. Avoid Junk Mail and Emails: Ignore junk mail and emails from unknown sources. Never click on links or provide information to telemarketers.

3. Verify Celebrity Claims: Celebrities endorsing products or financial advice may not be trustworthy. Conduct research before trusting celebrity-backed schemes.

4. Truths About Get Rich Quick Schemes: Understand the risks associated with get-rich-quick schemes. Most involve losing money, and guarantees are often deceptive.

5. Enhance your safety when selling valuable items: Opt for in-person meetings with buyers, avoid personal checks,

and carry a marker to authenticate dollar bills, preventing potential scams.

6. Use Strong Passwords: Craft strong, unique passwords for each account, steering clear of using the same one across multiple platforms. Regularly update your passwords to enhance their effectiveness. If you own an iPhone, refrain from noting down your passwords in the "Notes" section; opt for the dedicated Password option instead. Consider utilizing a reliable password manager like Dashlane, 1Password, or Keeper Password to generate and store complex passwords securely. Exercise caution, though, as even reputable companies may experience security breaches. For instance, LastPass faced a breach in August 2022, compromising users' password vaults. Stay vigilant and proactive in safeguarding your digital assets.

Remember, navigating financial challenges is a process. Stay informed, educate your family, and remain vigilant to protect yourself from scams. As scams evolve, ongoing awareness becomes your strongest defense against financial fraud and exploitation.

CHAPTER 21

BAD HABITS AND ADDICTIONS

Bad habits are repetitive, often unconscious behaviors that have negative consequences for one's well-being, productivity, and overall quality of life. They can manifest in various forms, affecting physical health, mental well-being, relationships, and, importantly, financial stability. Recognizing and addressing bad habits is a key step toward achieving financial freedom and responsible money management.

IDENTIFYING BAD HABITS:

Bad habits can infiltrate various aspects of our lives, making it vital to identify and understand them. Some common types of bad habits include:

1. Procrastination: Delaying tasks or decision-making can lead to missed opportunities and increased stress.

2. Impulse Spending: Unplanned and impulsive purchases can contribute significantly to financial strain.

3. Unhealthy Eating: Poor dietary choices and overeating can impact both physical health and medical expenses.

4. Excessive Screen Time: Spending excessive time on screens, whether for entertainment or social media, can hinder productivity and personal relationships.

5. Neglecting Exercise: A sedentary lifestyle has implications for physical health, potentially resulting in increased medical costs.

Addressing bad habits requires a proactive approach and commitment to change. Here are strategies to overcome common bad habits:

1. Set Clear Goals: Define specific, achievable goals to provide a sense of direction and purpose.

2. Create a Routine: Establishing a daily routine helps structure time and reduces the likelihood of succumbing to bad habits.

3. Seek Accountability: Share your goals with a friend or family member who can provide support and hold you accountable.

4. Replace with Positive Habits: Substitute bad habits with healthier alternatives. For instance, replace impulse spending with budgeting or saving.

5. Use Technology Wisely: Employ apps or tools that track and limit screen time, helping to break the cycle of excessive device use.

BAD HABITS vs. ADDICTIONS:

While bad habits and addictions share some similarities, addictions involve a stronger, often physiological dependence on a behavior or substance. Gambling, substance abuse, and excessive shopping can transition from bad habits to full-blown addictions.

UNDERSTANDING ADDICTIONS:

Addictions, unlike bad habits, are characterized by a loss of control and the inability to stop the behavior despite negative consequences. They often have a neurological basis, affecting the brain's reward and pleasure centers. Common addictions include:

1. Gambling Addiction: Compulsive gambling can lead to severe financial repercussions, impacting personal and familial well-being.

2. Substance Abuse: Drug or alcohol addiction can have far-reaching consequences on health, relationships, and financial stability.

3. Shopping Addiction: Excessive and compulsive shopping, often as a response to emotional distress, can result in overwhelming debt.

BREAKING FREE FROM ADDICTIONS:

Overcoming addiction is a complex process that often requires professional intervention. Here are the key steps:

1. Acknowledgment: Recognizing the addiction and its impact is the first crucial step towards recovery.

2. Seek Professional Help: Consult therapists, counselors, or support groups specializing in addiction treatment.

3. Establish Support Systems: Surround yourself with individuals who encourage positive change and provide emotional support.

4. Develop Coping Mechanisms: Identify healthier ways to cope with stress or emotional challenges, reducing reliance on addictive behaviors.

5. Curb Spending: Foster responsible financial habits by leaving credit cards at home, disabling one-click online shopping, avoiding malls with friends, using cash instead of cards, and sticking to a pre-set shopping list. Keep your budget and debt reduction goals in mind.

Addictions, especially those involving gambling or substance abuse, can wreak havoc on one's finances. Individuals may accumulate significant debt, experience job loss, and face legal consequences. Seeking financial guidance is essential to navigate these challenges and rebuild a stable economic foundation.

Breaking free from bad habits and addictions is a transformative journey that requires self-awareness, commitment, and often external support. By addressing these issues, individuals can redirect their focus toward responsible money management, ultimately paving the way for financial stability, debt reduction, and an improved quality of life.

CHAPTER 22

GAMBLING ADDICTION

Talking about bad habits and addictions, another significant problem in America is gambling, which notably jeopardizes efforts to escape debt. Gambling is a type of addiction similar to other forms like alcohol, drugs, or excessive use of social media. It involves a strong and harmful compulsion to regularly engage in activities like lottery tickets, scratch-offs, casinos, sports betting, and poker. The allure of quick riches often leads individuals into a financial abyss. The silent and deceptive nature of gambling addiction can drain finances, hindering progress toward debt reduction.

To address this issue, it's essential to recognize the addictive nature of gambling and take steps to become more aware of its impact, seeking support and taking measures to stop the harmful behavior.

TYPES OF GAMBLING:

Various types of gambling exist, with some being more popular than others. In America, common forms of gambling include lottery tickets, scratch-offs, casinos, bingo halls, racetracks, sports betting, poker, and other card games. These activities attract individuals seeking entertainment and a chance at financial gains, contributing to the widespread prevalence of gambling across the country.

DANGERS OF GAMBLING:

The dangers of gambling can have profound and wide-ranging impacts on individuals and their surroundings. Some of the key dangers include:

1. Financial Strain: Gambling can lead to severe financial problems, including debt, bankruptcy, and loss of assets. The allure of winning big can overshadow the financial risks involved, trapping individuals in a cycle of financial instability.

2. Addiction: Gambling can be highly addictive, leading to compulsive behavior and loss of control. Like other addictive substances, gambling can trigger changes in the brain's reward system, making individuals more susceptible to developing an addiction.

3. Emotional Distress: Losses in gambling can lead to emotional distress, including anxiety, depression, and

feelings of hopelessness. The emotional toll can strain relationships and impact overall mental well-being.

4. Relationship Issues: Gambling addiction can strain relationships with family and friends, leading to deceit, lies, and financial difficulties that erode trust and create conflicts within personal and professional relationships.

5. Legal Consequences: Excessive gambling can lead to legal issues, especially if individuals resort to illegal activities to fund their habit. Legal troubles, including criminal charges, can result in severe consequences.

6. Impact on Work and Education: Gambling addiction can interfere with work responsibilities and academic pursuits. Concentration difficulties, absenteeism, and decreased performance may result in job loss or academic failure.

7. Health Problems: The stress and anxiety associated with gambling problems can contribute to physical health issues, including insomnia, headaches, digestive problems, and other stress-related conditions.

8. Suicidal Thoughts: In severe cases, individuals grappling with the consequences of gambling addiction may experience thoughts of suicide. The overwhelming burden of financial issues and emotional distress can lead to desperate thoughts.

9. Family Breakdown: The strain caused by gambling problems can lead to family breakdowns, separations, or divorces. Children in the family may suffer emotional and psychological consequences.

10. Substance Abuse: Gambling addiction is often linked to an increased risk of substance abuse. Individuals may turn to drugs or alcohol as a way to cope with the stress and emotional turmoil caused by their gambling habits.

Understanding these dangers is pivotal for promoting awareness and encouraging responsible gambling behaviors. For those struggling with gambling-related issues, seeking help from support groups, counselors, or addiction specialists can be vital in overcoming challenges and reclaiming control over their lives.

ADDRESSING THE ISSUE OF GAMBLING:

Overcoming a gambling addiction is a challenging but necessary journey for individuals seeking positive change in their lives. Here are persuasive suggestions to help break free from the grips of gambling addiction:

1. Face the Reality: Acknowledge the problem and its impact on your life. Confronting the reality of the addiction is the first step towards recovery.

2. Seek Professional Help: Reach out to addiction specialists, therapists, or counselors who can provide

tailored guidance and support. Professional assistance is a valuable resource on the path to recovery.

3. Join Support Groups: Connect with others facing similar challenges through support groups like Gamblers Anonymous. Sharing experiences, struggles, and triumphs with a supportive community can be empowering.

4. Set Realistic Goals: Establish achievable goals for reducing and eventually eliminating gambling behavior. Celebrate small victories along the way, building momentum toward lasting change.

5. Develop Healthy Habits: Replace gambling activities with positive habits. Engage in activities that bring joy, fulfillment, and contribute to overall well-being. Cultivate a lifestyle that supports mental and physical health.

6. Install Barriers: Take practical steps to limit access to gambling opportunities. Self-exclusion programs, blocking online gambling sites, or banning yourself from casinos can create physical barriers to curb impulsive behavior.

7. Financial Management: Implement strict financial controls to prevent relapses. Establish budgets, limit

access to funds, and seek assistance in managing financial affairs responsibly.

8. Build a Support System: Surround yourself with a strong support system of friends and family. Open communication about your struggles fosters understanding and encourages a network of encouragement.

9. Educate Yourself: Gain knowledge about the psychology of gambling, addiction triggers, and recovery strategies. Watch videos on YouTube about how slot machines work and why the house always wins. Research on the internet about ways to cut out gambling addictions. Read books about others who have been through similar gambling addictions or read books about habits. According to James Clear's book "Atomic Habits," habits are built through four key stages: cue, craving, response, and reward. For a gambler, the sound of slot machines can trigger intense cravings, while non-gamblers perceive it as background noise. To break a bad habit, modify the four laws: (Cue) Make it invisible, (Craving) Make it unattractive, (Response) Make it difficult, and (Reward) Make it unsatisfying. For example, a gambler can eliminate the visual cues of casinos, find the unattractive aspects of gambling, make it logistically difficult to gamble, and associate it with unsatisfying

outcomes. Gaining a deep understanding of the challenges posed by a gambling addiction and incorporating healthy habits into your life can pave the way for more informed and smarter choices in the future.

10. Celebrate Progress: Recognize and celebrate milestones in your journey. Whether it's a week, a month, or a year without gambling, each achievement is a testament to your resilience and determination.

Breaking free from a gambling addiction is a vital step in the journey toward financial responsibility. It's a challenging process that demands commitment and perseverance. By acknowledging the issue, seeking support, and cultivating healthier habits, individuals pave the way for a debt-free and financially responsible future, ultimately transforming their relationship with money for the better.

CHAPTER 23

BEING FRUGAL

Frugality is not just a way of managing money; it's a lifestyle that centers on mindful spending, resourcefulness, and the pursuit of financial sustainability. Living a frugal life involves making deliberate choices to spend less, prioritize needs over wants, and avoid unnecessary debt. It's about finding contentment and fulfillment without succumbing to the pressure of consumerism and extravagant spending. Embracing frugality is not a sacrifice; it's a strategic and empowering approach to life that can lead to financial freedom and a more peaceful existence.

At its core, frugality revolves around the concept of spending less than you earn. It's a mindset shift that challenges the societal norms of constant consumption and the pursuit of material possessions. Frugal individuals are not necessarily miserly or stingy; instead, they are intentional about their spending, seeking value and quality in their purchases. Frugality encourages making conscious decisions about where your money goes, tracking expenses, and setting financial goals.

HERE ARE THE KEY PRINCIPLES THAT DEFINE AND GUIDE A FRUGAL LIFESTYLE:

1. Mindful Spending: Frugal living begins with an awareness of where your money goes. By understanding your spending habits, you can make informed decisions that align with your financial goals.

2. Prioritizing Your Dollars: Your money is like an army of soldiers. Frugal living means directing them toward the battles that matter most. Identify your financial goals, whether it's paying off debt, saving for a dream vacation, or investing for the future, and allocate your resources accordingly.

3. Resourceful Living: It's about being resourceful, finding creative solutions, and reusing what you have before rushing to the store. This not only saves money but also minimizes waste.

4. Waste Not, Want Not: Minimizing waste is a cornerstone of frugal living. Whether it's food, energy, or time, frugal individuals aim to use everything efficiently. Leftovers become tomorrow's lunch, lights are turned off when leaving a room, and every resource is valued.

5. Quality Over Quantity: Frugal living doesn't mean settling for cheap, low-quality items. It's about getting the best value for your money. Investing in durable and high-

quality goods, even if they cost more upfront, can save money in the long run by avoiding frequent replacements.

6. Living a Fulfilling Life: Perhaps the most compelling aspect of frugal living is that it's not about deprivation. Frugal individuals still savor life's pleasures but in a way that aligns with their values and financial goals. It's about enjoying experiences and possessions in moderation, without breaking the bank.

WHY FRUGALITY MATTERS:

1. Debt Reduction: One of the primary reasons to embrace frugality is to get out of debt. Frugal living plays a crucial role in managing your finances and getting rid of debts. It involves making wise choices, cutting unnecessary expenses, and strategically allocating your funds. Adopting a frugal lifestyle can expedite your journey to a debt-free life and avoid accumulating more financial burdens.

2. Financial Freedom: Frugality is a pathway to financial freedom. Individuals can build a financial cushion that provides security and freedom by spending less, saving more, and making informed financial decisions. Financial independence means having the flexibility to pursue dreams, make career changes, or retire comfortably.

3. Reduced Stress: Financial stress is a pervasive issue, and living beyond one's means can lead to constant worry and fear. Frugal living helps individuals take control of their finances, reducing stress and anxiety associated with money matters. The peace of mind that comes with financial stability is a significant benefit of embracing a frugal lifestyle.

4. Sustainable Living: Frugality aligns with principles of sustainability. By minimizing waste, reusing items, and making environmentally conscious choices, frugal individuals contribute to a more sustainable and eco-friendly lifestyle. This not only benefits the individual but also has positive implications for the planet.

5. Increased Savings: Frugality encourages a disciplined approach to saving money. Whether it's for emergencies, future investments, or retirement, the habit of saving consistently is a key component of frugal living. Increased savings provide a safety net and open up opportunities for wealth-building.

6. Conscious Consumption: In a world dominated by consumerism, frugality promotes conscious consumption. It encourages individuals to question the necessity of purchases, resist impulse buying, and focus on what truly adds value to their lives. This shift in

mindset fosters a more intentional and fulfilling way of living.

HOW TO EMBRACE A FRUGAL LIFESTYLE:

1. Set Clear Financial Goals: Begin by defining your financial objectives. Whether it's paying off debt, building an emergency fund, or saving for a specific goal, clear goals serve as a roadmap for your frugal journey.

2. Create a Budget: A budget is an essential tool for frugal living. List your monthly income and expenses, and allocate funds wisely to prioritize your financial goals. Regularly review and adjust your budget as needed.

3. Wage War on Debt: Actively work towards paying off outstanding debts. Channeling more money into debt repayment means less is spent on interest and more is available for savings and investments.

4. Hunt for Deals: Be a savvy shopper. Look for discounts, coupons, and sales when making purchases. Consider thrift stores and borrowing items from friends and family before buying new ones.

5. Trim Unnecessary Expenses: Identify areas where you can cut unnecessary expenses. Whether it's dining out, subscription services, or impulse purchases, trimming these costs can significantly impact your budget.

6. DIY Repairs and Maintenance: Learn basic repairs to avoid costly professional services. Regular maintenance can prevent future expenses. Repurpose and reuse items to reduce the need for new purchases.

7. Energy Efficiency: Invest in energy-efficient appliances and practices to save on utility bills. Conserving resources and reducing waste align with both frugality and sustainability.

8. Mindful Grocery Shopping: Plan meals, create shopping lists, and avoid impulse purchases. Buying in bulk and taking advantage of sales can also contribute to significant savings.

9. Prioritize Quality Over Quantity: Invest in durable, high-quality items that may have a higher upfront cost but offer long-term value. This approach avoids frequent replacements and ultimately saves money.

10. Live Within Your Means: Avoid the temptation to keep up with trends or societal expectations. Live within your means, focus on your financial goals, and resist unnecessary expenditures.

In a world that often encourages excessive spending and instant gratification, embracing frugality is a powerful choice that can lead to financial stability, reduced stress, and a more intentional and fulfilling life. By prioritizing mindful spending, resourcefulness, and sustainability, individuals can break free from the cycle of debt, build a secure financial future, and contribute to a healthier and more balanced way of living. Frugality is not about sacrificing joy; it's about finding joy in a life aligned with one's values and long-term goals.

CHAPTER 24

DISCIPLINE

The financial crisis of 2008-2009 and the COVID-19 pandemic served as wake-up calls for many households, forcing them to confront the fragility of their financial lives. The sudden economic downturns led to widespread job losses, decreased property values, and heightened financial uncertainty. Individuals and families who once relied on stable incomes and assumed financial security found themselves grappling with unexpected challenges.

These crises underscored the importance of being frugal and practicing financial discipline. Many households were caught off guard, having overextended themselves with debts and living beyond their means. These shocks prompted a reevaluation of spending habits, savings, and overall financial preparedness for countless individuals and families.

Being frugal in times of economic stability and discipline in financial management are important for several reasons:

1. Emergency Preparedness: Frugality involves building a financial cushion through savings. This buffer can serve as a lifeline during unexpected crises, covering essential expenses when income is disrupted.

2. Reduced Debt Burden: Frugal living encourages individuals to avoid unnecessary debts and manage existing ones responsibly. A lower debt burden provides greater flexibility during economic downturns, reducing financial stress.

3. Adaptability to Changing Circumstances: Financial discipline allows flexibility in adapting to changing circumstances. Frugal individuals are better equipped to adjust their lifestyles, cut non-essential expenses, and weather financial storms.

4. Long-Term Financial Resilience: The ability to live within one's means, save consistently, and invest wisely contributes to long-term financial resilience. Frugality establishes a solid foundation for future financial well-being.

5. Mindful Spending: Frugality promotes mindful spending, encouraging individuals to differentiate between essential needs and discretionary wants. This mindset

fosters a more deliberate approach to financial decisions.

6. Learning from Crises: Experiencing financial crises can serve as powerful lessons. Those who emerge from such challenges with a commitment to frugality and financial discipline are more likely to avoid repeating past mistakes.

7. Building a Sustainable Lifestyle: Frugal living is not solely about cutting costs; it's about building a sustainable lifestyle that aligns with one's financial goals. This sustainable approach minimizes the risk of falling into financial traps during turbulent times.

8. Preparing for the Unforeseen: Unforeseen events, such as economic recessions or global pandemics, can have far-reaching consequences. Being frugal ensures that individuals are better prepared for the unexpected, reducing vulnerability.

In essence, the financial crises of the past serve as reminders that economic stability is not guaranteed. By embracing frugality and practicing financial discipline, individuals can fortify themselves against unforeseen challenges, secure their financial futures, and navigate uncertainties with greater resilience.

Becoming more disciplined with time and money while adopting a frugal mindset involves incorporating specific strategies into your daily life. Here are some steps to help you achieve greater discipline:

SET CLEAR GOALS:

1. Define your short-term and long-term financial goals.

2. Create a Budget: Develop a detailed budget outlining your income, expenses, and savings goals. Categorize your spending to identify areas where you can cut back.

3. Track Your Spending: Monitor your daily expenses to gain insight into your spending habits. Use budgeting apps or spreadsheets to help you keep a close eye on your financial transactions.

4. Prioritize Needs Over Wants: Distinguish between essential needs and discretionary wants. Focus on satisfying your needs before indulging in non-essential purchases.

5. Use Cash Instead of Cards: Withdraw a set amount of cash for discretionary spending each week. Using physical cash can make you more conscious of your expenditures.

6. Automate Savings: Set up automatic transfers to your savings account each month. Treat savings as a non-negotiable expense to build financial discipline.

7. Practice Delayed Gratification: Avoid impulsive purchases by implementing a waiting period before buying non-essential items. Consider whether the purchase aligns with your financial goals.

8. Time Blocking: Schedule specific blocks of time for various activities, including work, leisure, and personal development. Stick to your designated time blocks to enhance productivity and time management.

9. Limit Exposure to Ads: Reduce exposure to advertisements. Unsubscribe from marketing emails and limit time on platforms that promote impulsive buying.

10. Educate Yourself: Increase financial literacy by reading books, attending workshops, or taking online courses. Learn about budgeting, investing, and other financial strategies.

11. Surround Yourself with Like-Minded Individuals: Engage with people who share similar financial and time-management values. Share experiences and learn from others who have successfully adopted disciplined habits. Similar to weight loss, overcoming financial challenges requires a disciplined approach, which may include cutting ties with those who delay your progress.

12. Review and Adjust: Regularly review your budget and financial goals. Adjust your strategies based on changes in income, expenses, or priorities.

13. Embrace a Minimalist Mindset: Evaluate your possessions and focus on quality over quantity. Declutter your life, both physically and financially, to reduce unnecessary burdens.

14. Seek Accountability: Share your financial and time management goals with a trusted friend or family member. Regular check-ins can provide motivation and accountability.

15. Celebrate Small Wins: Acknowledge and celebrate your achievements, no matter how small. Rewarding yourself for reaching milestones can reinforce positive habits.

By incorporating these steps into your daily routine, you can develop greater discipline with your time and money, ultimately leading to a more frugal and purposeful lifestyle. Discipline, strategic choices, and a redefined view of wealth are crucial in overcoming debt and achieving financial security.

CHAPTER 25

LEARN TO NEGOTIATE

Negotiating is an art and a skill that involves discussions and compromise between two or more parties to reach a mutually beneficial agreement. While negotiating is common in many cultures worldwide, it's not as ingrained in American culture, where fixed prices and advertised costs are prevalent. However, understanding and practicing negotiation can be a powerful tool for individuals to save money on various purchases, from small items at garage sales to significant investments like buying a house.

Negotiation is not just about haggling over prices but also about understanding the needs, motivations, and constraints of both parties involved. Successful negotiation often results in a win-win scenario, where both sides feel satisfied with the outcome.

IMPORTANCE OF NEGOTIATION:

1. Saving Money: Negotiating allows individuals to secure better deals and discounts, potentially saving significant amounts of money. Whether buying a used item, negotiating a salary, or purchasing a home, the ability to haggle can lead to substantial financial benefits.

2. Building Relationships: Negotiation is not solely about the transaction; it's also about building relationships. A positive negotiation experience can foster trust and respect between parties, creating a foundation for future interactions.

3. Problem-Solving: Negotiation involves creative problem-solving. It encourages individuals to think outside the box, explore alternatives, and find innovative solutions to meet the needs of all parties involved.

4. Confidence Building: Mastering negotiation builds confidence. The more individuals practice and succeed in negotiations, the more self-assured they become in various aspects of their personal and professional lives.

5. Empowerment: Negotiation empowers individuals to advocate for themselves and their interests. It shifts the power dynamic from a one-sided decision to a collaborative process where both parties have a say.

PRACTICAL APPLICATIONS OF NEGOTIATION:

1. Garage Sales and Flea Markets: Approach sellers politely and express interest in multiple items. Bundle purchases for a better deal, emphasizing bulk buying. Point out any flaws or imperfections to negotiate a lower price.

2. Retail Purchases: Inquire about discounts, especially for floor models or display items. Mention competitor prices to leverage better deals. Be willing to walk away if the seller is not open to negotiation.

3. Salary Negotiation: Research industry salary standards for the position. Highlight achievements and skills that justify a higher salary. Negotiate additional benefits or perks if a salary increase is challenging.

4. Real Estate Transactions: Research the local housing market to understand property values. Identify any issues or needed repairs to negotiate a lower price. Be patient and prepared to counteroffer during the negotiation process.

5. Car Purchases: Research the fair market value of the desired vehicle. Be prepared to negotiate the price, financing terms, and additional features. Consider getting pre-approved for a loan to strengthen negotiation positions.

Negotiation is a valuable skill that can empower individuals to save money, build relationships, and navigate various aspects of life more effectively. While it may not be as ingrained in American culture as in some other societies, learning and practicing negotiation can lead to numerous benefits. Whether bargaining at a garage sale, negotiating a salary, or closing a real estate deal, mastering the art of negotiation is a valuable investment in personal and financial success.

CHAPTER 26

DO IT YOURSELF (DIY)

Embracing a do-it-yourself lifestyle not only helps in saving money but also empowers individuals to take control of various aspects of their lives. Whether it's home improvement, personal grooming, or financial tasks, the satisfaction of accomplishing these projects on your own contributes to both financial resilience and a sense of self-reliance. As you master different skills, the benefits extend beyond cost savings, fostering a greater sense of independence and resourcefulness.

Here are various ways individuals can practice Do It Yourself (DIY) to save money:

1. Home Repairs:
   - Fix minor plumbing issues like leaks or clogs.
   - Patch small holes or cracks in walls.
   - Repair or replace leaky faucets.
   - Install shelves or other simple storage solutions.

- Paint rooms or furniture.

2. Cleaning:
   - Clean your own home instead of hiring a service.
   - Do your own carpet cleaning.
   - Wash your car instead of going to a car wash.

3. Gardening and Yard Work:
   - Mow your lawn instead of hiring a service.
   - Plant and maintain your own garden.
   - Trim trees and bushes.

4. Vehicle Maintenance:
   - Learn to change your car's oil.
   - Rotate your own tires.
   - Replace air filters or spark plugs.

5. Cooking and Food Preparation:
   - Cook meals at home instead of dining out.
   - Bake your own bread, cookies, or other treats.
   - Make your own coffee or tea.

6. Clothing and Fashion:
   - Mend or repair torn clothing.
   - Sew buttons or make basic alterations.
   - Create your own fashion accessories.

7. Technology and Electronics:
   - Troubleshoot and fix minor issues with electronic devices.

- Build or upgrade your own computer.
- Install software or perform basic computer maintenance.

8. Financial Tasks:

- Prepare your own taxes using online tools.
- Create your own budget and financial plan.
- Learn to invest on your own.

9. Event Planning:

- Make your own party decorations.
- Create DIY invitations for events.
- Prepare homemade gifts for occasions.

10. Health and Beauty:

- Do your own manicures and pedicures.
- Invest in at-home waxing kits.
- Learn to apply false eyelashes at home instead of paying for salon treatments.
- Try DIY haircuts or styling.
- Avoid salons for hair coloring and buy a home kit as an alternative.

11. Crafts and Hobbies:

- Make your own home décor.
- Craft personalized gifts.
- Learn a new craft or skill.

12. Education:

- Take advantage of online resources for learning.

- DIY home improvement projects with help from tutorials.
- Join DIY workshops or classes.

13. Gifts and Presents:
    - Create handmade gifts for special occasions.
    - Design your own greeting cards.
    - Build custom gift baskets.

14. Pet Care:
    - Groom your pets at home.
    - Make your own pet toys.
    - Walk your dog yourself versus paying someone to do it.

Remember, starting small and gradually expanding your DIY skills can lead to significant savings and a sense of accomplishment. DIY is an excellent way to embrace frugality and pocket substantial savings.

CHAPTER 27

RENT VS BUYING A HOME

For countless Americans, owning a home is viewed as achieving the American Dream. However, the dream often conceals a web of hidden costs and maintenance responsibilities that can catch new homeowners off guard. Let's unravel the complexities, examine the surprise elements, and explore the benefits of renting versus buying.

1. Hidden Costs of Homeownership:

   - Down Payment: While having enough money saved up for a down payment is great, it's not the only cash you'll need to seal the deal on a home purchase.

   - Private Mortgage Insurance (PMI): A type of mortgage insurance you might be required to buy if you take out a conventional loan with a down payment of less than 20 percent of the purchase price. PMI protects the lender—not you—if you stop making payments.

- Closing Costs: Appraisals, inspections, and administrative fees can total thousands.
- Home Insurance: Typically, homeowners' insurance premiums can be paid monthly or in a lump sum annually.
- Property Taxes: Often overlooked, these recur annually and may increase.

2. Maintenance Expenses:

- Homeowners face unforeseen expenses, from leaky roofs to malfunctioning appliances.
- The burden of maintenance can strain the budget unexpectedly.
- Renters enjoy landlord-managed repairs.

3. Market Volatility:

- Unpredictable real estate markets can depreciate property values.
- Economic downturns may impact the resale value, challenging the view of homeownership as an investment.
- Market fluctuations can lead to financial losses rather than gains.

4. Debt Dilemmas:

- Debt Holders Beware: Carrying debt before buying? Brace for unforeseen financial shocks.

- Big Projects, Bigger Bills: From roofs to driveways to fences, massive expenses can disrupt financial stability.

5. Advantages of Renting:

- Flexibility and Mobility: Renting allows for easier relocation without the complexities of selling.

- Financial Predictability: Shielded from immediate and unexpected financial shocks of homeownership.

- Hassle-Free Lifestyle: Repairs and maintenance are the landlord's responsibility.

6. Financial Realities:

- Costs associated with selling a home can offset potential equity gains, especially for short-term owners.

- Renting provides a level of financial predictability, shielding from the uncertainties of homeownership.

- The transient nature of modern careers aligns with renting, offering freedom from long-term commitments.

7. Societal Pressures:

- Despite the benefits of renting, societal pressures to own a home persist.

- Individuals often feel compelled to follow the traditional path without evaluating practical alternatives.

- Opt for renting. Choose a lifestyle that embraces freedom, not just a title deed.

In the pursuit of homeownership, understanding hidden costs and long-term commitments is paramount. Renting emerges as a compelling alternative for those prioritizing flexibility, financial predictability, and a maintenance-free lifestyle. Dispel the myth that owning a home is the sole path to financial stability, allowing individuals to make informed housing choices aligned with their unique circumstances and goals.

CHAPTER 28

PREVENTION AND MAINTENANCE

P reventative maintenance for cars and homes is essential to save money by addressing issues before they become expensive problems. Regular maintenance helps identify potential issues early, allowing for timely and cost-effective repairs. For cars, tasks like tire rotations, fluid changes, and filter replacements prevent major breakdowns, ensuring the vehicle's longevity and avoiding costly repairs. Similarly, in homes, tasks such as addressing drafts, inspecting HVAC systems, and maintaining appliances prevent expensive repairs and energy inefficiencies. Investing in preventative maintenance is a proactive approach that ultimately saves money by avoiding the need for major repairs or replacements down the line.

PREVENTATIVE MAINTENANCE FOR VEHICLES:

Maintaining your vehicle through regular preventative measures is essential for ensuring its longevity and cost-efficient operation. Neglecting these tasks can lead to expensive repairs and breakdowns. By investing in preventative maintenance, you can avoid significant issues down the road. Here are key maintenance tasks you should consider:

Every 6 Months:

1. Rotate Your Tires: Tires wear down differently based on their position. Regular rotations every six months or 6,000 to 8,000 miles help ensure even wear and extend tire life.

2. Balance and Align Wheels: Routine balancing and alignment every 6,000 miles or six months distribute weight evenly, preventing tire wobbling and improving fuel efficiency.

Every 6 to 12 Months:

1. Install New Windshield Wipers: Replace windshield wipers every six months or when they fail to maintain proper contact, ensuring clear visibility during adverse weather conditions.

Every 3 to 5 Years:

1. Clean and Test Your Battery: Regular battery testing and maintenance, along with DIY terminal cleaning, can prevent unexpected dead batteries, offering peace of mind and ensuring your vehicle starts reliably.

Every 30,000 Miles:

1. Replace Spark Plugs: Change spark plugs every 30,000 miles to ensure proper ignition and maintain your vehicle's performance.

At Various Mileage Intervals:

Change Interior/Exterior Filters:

1. Air Filter: Replace every 30-40,000 miles or as per manufacturer specifications.

2. Cabin Air Filter: Replace every 15-20,000 miles or annually.

3. Fuel Filter: Replace every 20-40,000 miles or according to manufacturer specifications.

Regularly replacing these filters is essential to maintain optimal engine performance.

Remember, preventative maintenance helps catch problems early and avoid unexpected repairs, saving you money in the long run.

PREVENTATIVE MAINTENANCE FOR HOMES:

A home is a significant investment, and regular maintenance is necessary to protect it and prevent costly repairs. Here are some tips for home preventative maintenance:

1. Invest in Basic Tools: Assemble a basic home toolkit comprising essentials like a toolbox, cordless drill, stud finder, hammer, nails, screws, wrenches, and pliers, ensuring you're equipped for common household repairs and projects.

2. Save Leftover Materials: Store leftover screws, bolts, and small hardware in a container to avoid unnecessary trips to the hardware store and save money on minor fixes.

Preventive Maintenance Tips:

1. Address Drafts: Plug leaks to reduce heating and cooling bills.

2. Furnace and Water Heater Maintenance: Change furnace filters every three months and have them inspected annually. Inspect your water heater regularly.

3. Insulate Pipes: Prevent freezing by insulating pipes during winter.

4. Vegetation Clearance: Clear vegetation around your air conditioner to extend its lifespan.

5. Attic Vent Inspection: Check vents for cracks and patch them with foil tape to improve HVAC system efficiency.

6. Water Heater Drainage: Drain your water heater annually to prevent sediment buildup.

7. Roof Inspection: Check for loose roof shingles and secure them with roof cement.

Ultimately, home maintenance will always be something you need to periodically take on. Preventative home maintenance tasks can save you money and protect your home. Regular inspections and timely repairs can prevent costly issues and maintain your home's value.

CHAPTER 29

REDUCE,

REUSE, RECYCLE

In the United States, we face a significant challenge with too much waste production. Our habit of quickly discarding items after brief use depletes natural resources, harms the environment, and contributes to pollution. To address this issue, it's important to understand and practice the "three Rs" — reduce, reuse, and recycle. These principles offer effective strategies for minimizing the environmental impact of waste and working towards a sustainable future. By embracing these practices, each of us can contribute to a healthier planet by making mindful choices and reducing our ecological footprint.

REDUCE:

The first step in waste reduction involves a conscious effort to minimize waste generation. Americans can start by making mindful choices while shopping. Purchasing products with minimal packaging or opting for items in bulk reduces the overall waste associated with packaging materials. Choosing durable, long-lasting goods instead of disposable ones offers a dual benefit: it not only decreases waste but also results in long-term financial savings. This choice actively diminishes the demand for raw materials, thereby lowering the environmental impact linked to extraction and manufacturing processes. Furthermore, adopting a minimalist lifestyle and refraining from unnecessary purchases significantly reduces resource demand and, consequently, the overall production of waste.

REUSE:

Reusing items is a powerful strategy to extend the lifespan of products and diminish the need for constant replacements. Americans can adopt a more circular approach to consumption by finding creative ways to reuse items in their daily lives. For example, repurposing glass jars for storage, using cloth bags instead of disposable ones, or refurbishing old furniture instead of discarding it are simple yet effective ways to practice reuse. Thrift stores, consignment shops, and online platforms for secondhand goods offer opportunities to give pre-loved items a new lease on life. By prioritizing reuse, individuals contribute to a culture of sustainability and reduce the burden on landfills.

RECYCLE:

Proper recycling is a key element in waste management. Americans should familiarize themselves with local recycling programs and guidelines to ensure that materials are sorted and disposed of correctly. Common recyclables include paper, cardboard, plastic, glass, and metal. Additionally, electronic waste, such as old smartphones and computers, should be taken to designated e-waste recycling facilities. Participating in community recycling initiatives and encouraging others to do the same can amplify the positive impact.

CONSUMER RESPONSIBILITY:

Individuals can take a proactive role in promoting sustainability by supporting businesses committed to eco-friendly practices. Choosing products made from recycled materials creates demand for a closed-loop system, where materials are continually recycled into new products. Avoiding single-use plastics and embracing reusable alternatives, such as water bottles and coffee cups, can significantly reduce the environmental footprint associated with disposable items. By making informed choices, consumers send a powerful message to industries to prioritize environmentally conscious practices.

In conclusion, combating landfill waste in America necessitates a united effort to reduce, reuse, and recycle. Integrating these principles into daily life allows Americans to actively contribute to a sustainable future, conserving natural resources, curbing pollution, and fostering a healthier environment for present and future generations. This collective responsibility begins with individual actions and extends to broader community initiatives, molding a nation that esteems and safeguards its environment while minimizing the impact of waste.

Embracing the principles of reduce, reuse, and recycle is not just an environmental responsibility but a strategic choice for those pursuing a frugal lifestyle, fostering resourcefulness and maximizing the value of every item. By consciously limiting consumption (reduce), maximizing existing resources (reuse), and ensuring responsible waste disposal (recycle), individuals can have a significant impact on both their finances and the environment. Choosing durability and quality over frequent replacements aligns with frugal living, resulting in long-term financial savings. Additionally, recycling contributes to the circular economy, lessening the demand for new raw materials. Living frugally through these practices is a small yet impactful way for individuals to positively influence both personal financial goals and environmental sustainability.

CHAPTER 30

LOVE AND FINANCES

Before embarking on the journey of marriage or cohabitation, it is key to gain insight into your partner's financial habits. Take the time to date and live together, allowing a firsthand observation of how your partner handles money. This period of coexistence serves as a valuable prelude to making a lifelong commitment. Living together provides a unique opportunity to identify any potential warning signs regarding how your partner manages finances.

1. The Wisdom of Observation:

    *   Money Management: Watch how your partner handles day-to-day finances, offering valuable insights into their money management skills.

- Spending Habits: Observe spending patterns to understand their approach towards expenses and financial decision-making.

- Financial Priorities: Take note of where your partner allocates their financial resources, revealing their priorities and values.

- Debt Handling: Assess how your partner deals with debts, providing vital information about their financial responsibility.

- Long-Term Goals: Discuss and observe their perspectives on long-term financial goals, ensuring alignment for a harmonious future.

- Saving Practices: Explore their saving habits and understand their attitude towards building financial security.

- Being opposite: While it's often said that opposites attract, when it comes to finances, having contrasting money habits—such as being a saver while your partner is a spender—can lead to significant challenges down the road.

- Communication about Finances: Note how comfortably your partner communicates about money matters, fostering transparency in the relationship.

2. Potential Pitfalls of Ignoring Financial Red Flags:

- Credit Troubles: Joint accounts impact both partners' credit reports, jeopardizing your ability to qualify for loans or buy a home.

- Financial Struggles: Discrepancies in money management can strain relationships, adding pressure to pay bills and navigate disagreements.

- Debt Repayment Woes: Excessive spending by a partner may lead to a lifetime of debt repayment, consuming disposable income.

- Hidden Money Problems: Unveiling your partner's undisclosed financial issues, from gambling addictions to severe debt, can be a harsh reality.

3. Why Pre-Marital Financial Discussions Matter:

- Medical Debt and Bankruptcies: Essential questions about past financial struggles, bankruptcies, and medical debt must be addressed.

- Investment Portfolio: Understanding your partner's investment philosophy and portfolio can align future financial goals.

- Financial Priorities: Divergent views on saving for education versus retirement, along with insurance coverage details, should be discussed.

- Spending Habits: Assessing your partner's saving tendencies, attitude towards debt, current consumer debt, and retirement savings is essential.

4. Avoiding Financial Disasters:

- Ask the Right Questions: Valerie emphasizes asking about assets, debts, and financial details to avoid surprises.

- Context Matters: Understand the context of your partner's financial situation—past mistakes may not define their current intentions.

- Desire for Change: Assess whether your partner is genuinely committed to changing their financial habits for a better future.

While everyone's financial journey is unique, entering a union without essential discussions can lead to avoidable hardships. Choosing a life partner involves more than just love; financial compatibility is a critical component. Don't let love blindside you to financial realities. Before making a lifelong commitment, take the time to date and live together, observing how your partner manages money. A partner with sound financial habits contributes positively to shared goals, easing the journey through life's challenges. Choose wisely because love should make life better, not harder. As the saying goes, "for better or for worse, for richer or for poorer," life's challenges become more manageable when both partners are fully aware of what they are stepping into.

CHAPTER 31

SAVING ON EVENTS

Navigating events on a frugal path requires thoughtful planning and a dose of creativity. When it comes to events such as weddings, funerals, holidays, and birthdays, being financially conscious doesn't mean missing out; it means finding resourceful ways to participate without breaking the bank.

WEDDINGS:

1. Gift Alternatives: Instead of an expensive gift, consider offering your time or skills. Craft a personalized, handmade item or volunteer to help with wedding preparations.

2. Attire: Opt for outfits you already own or explore affordable second-hand options. Skip the designer duds and still look stylish.

3. Travel: If you're invited to a wedding that's far away and you can't afford to travel, it's okay to politely decline the invitation. Instead, consider sending a heartfelt card and a small gift to celebrate their special day. If the couple isn't very close to you, you can simply send them well wishes on social media. Remember, you don't have to attend every event if it doesn't fit your budget or financial goals, especially if you're working on paying off debt.

Getting married and planning a wedding can quickly become expensive, particularly if you opt for the traditional route of hosting both a wedding ceremony and reception. Costs can escalate depending on factors such as the number of bridesmaids and groomsmen, as well as the chosen location. The planning of a wedding alone can be stressful, especially if you're already dealing with a lot of debt.

However, there are several simple ways to have a beautiful wedding without breaking the bank.

1. Set a Realistic Budget: Begin by establishing a realistic budget based on what you can afford, considering your current financial situation. Determine the maximum amount you're willing to spend on each aspect of the wedding.

2. Prioritize Your Expenses: Identify the most important elements of your wedding and allocate a larger portion of your budget to those areas. Whether it's the venue,

photography, or entertainment, focus your resources on the aspects of the wedding that matter most to you and your partner.

3. Consider Non-Traditional Venues: Explore alternative venue options such as parks, beaches, or community centers, which may offer more affordable rental rates compared to traditional wedding venues. Look for venues that allow you to bring in your own vendors or offer package deals to save on costs.

4. DIY Decor and Invitations: Get creative and make your own wedding decorations, centerpieces, and invitations to save on expenses. Utilize resources such as online tutorials, craft stores, and printable templates to create personalized touches for your wedding without spending a fortune.

5. Opt for Off-Peak Dates and Times: Consider scheduling your wedding during off-peak months or on weekdays, as venues and vendors may offer discounted rates during these times. Hosting a brunch or afternoon wedding can also be more budget-friendly than an evening affair.

6. Limit the Guest List: Keep your guest list small and intimate to reduce costs associated with catering, seating, and favors. Focus on inviting close family and friends who are truly important to you rather than feeling obligated to invite everyone you know.

7. Simplify the Menu: Choose a simple and budget-friendly menu that reflects your personal preferences and dietary restrictions. Consider alternatives to a traditional sit-down dinner, such as buffet-style, which can be a more affordable option.

8. Borrow or Rent Attire: Instead of purchasing brand-new wedding attire, consider borrowing or renting wedding attire for you and your bridal party. Look for bridal shops or online rental services that offer designer dresses and suits at a fraction of the cost of buying new ones.

9. Limit Alcohol Options: Opt for a limited selection of beer, wine, and signature cocktails to keep bar costs in check. Consider offering a cash bar or providing a limited number of drink tickets per guest to control alcohol expenses.

10. DIY Music Playlist: Create your own wedding playlist and use a sound system, or hire a DJ for a more budget-friendly alternative to live music or bands. Compile a mix of your favorite songs and crowd-pleasers to keep guests entertained throughout the reception.

By implementing these frugal methods and prioritizing your wedding expenses, you can have a memorable and meaningful celebration without adding to your existing debt. Focus on what truly matters to you as a couple and find creative ways to make your wedding day special within your budget constraints.

Keep in mind that a wedding is just a one-day ceremony. If you create a checklist and tally up the costs of each aspect—like catering, attire, and decorations—you may be surprised at how quickly expenses accumulate. If you're already in debt, it's wise to reconsider your options before diving into wedding planning. Remind yourself that it's only a one-day event.

FUNERALS:

1. Similar to wedding invitations, you don't have to feel obligated to attend every funeral, especially if it involves significant travel expenses and you're focused on paying off debt. Instead, consider making a phone call to offer your condolences. Prioritize your financial goals while still showing your support and care in a meaningful way.

2. Condolence Cards: Express your sympathy with a heartfelt card. Offer your support and words of comfort, and consider sharing fond memories.

3. Minimal Expenses: Attend the funeral without incurring unnecessary costs. Focus on being present and supportive rather than lavish gestures.

HOLIDAYS:

1. Gift Exchanges: Suggest a gift exchange among family or friends to keep expenses in check. Set reasonable spending limits to ensure everyone can participate.

2. Potluck Dinners: Host a potluck-style gathering where each guest contributes a dish. It spreads the financial responsibility and adds a communal touch to the celebration. Make this an annual tradition for holidays such as Thanksgiving or Christmas.

3. Avoid Celebrating: Many Americans spend money on unnecessary holidays, some of which may not even resonate with them culturally. For example, it's not essential to splurge on St. Patrick's Day or Cinco de Mayo, especially if these celebrations aren't part of your cultural background. Don't feel pressured to spend money on numerous holidays when you're striving to get out of debt. Focus on your financial priorities and allocate your resources wisely.

BIRTHDAYS:

1. DIY Gifts: Craft a personalized, meaningful gift instead of purchasing an expensive one. Handwritten letters, photo collages, or homemade treats showcase thoughtfulness.

2. Group Celebrations: Instead of individual gifts, pool resources for a joint celebration. It's a cost-effective way to honor the birthday person without overspending.

OTHER EVENTS:

1. Prioritize: Evaluate event invitations and prioritize attendance based on your budget. It's okay to decline some and attend those that matter most.

2. Virtual Participation: When distance or financial constraints arise, consider virtually joining events through video calls. You can share your best wishes without incurring travel expenses.

GENERAL TIPS:

1. Plan Ahead: Anticipate upcoming events and budget accordingly. Planning allows you to allocate funds wisely and avoid last-minute financial stress.

2. DIY Decorations: Save on costs by crafting your decorations for events you host, adding a personal touch without breaking the bank.

3. Free Events: Explore local free events or activities. Many communities offer concerts, festivals, or gatherings that provide entertainment without a hefty price tag.

Being frugal doesn't mean missing out on significant life events; it's about redefining participation. By thoughtfully choosing when and how to engage, you can navigate these occasions with financial wisdom. Embrace the joy of simplicity, and let meaningful connections take precedence over extravagant expenses.

CHAPTER 32

SAVE WHILE PARENTING

In America, raising a child can be super expensive, and many individuals may not realize all the costs involved. From prenatal care to education and everyday expenses, it adds up fast. Learning how to budget, save, and make wise financial choices can help lighten the financial load of raising a child.

Here are a few tips to help save money while parenting:

1. Buy Secondhand: Opt for gently-used baby clothes, toys, and gear. Thrift stores, consignment shops, and online marketplaces can offer affordable alternatives.

2. Breastfeeding: If possible, breastfeeding is not only beneficial for the child's health but also eliminates the need to spend money on formula.

3. DIY Baby Food: Making your own baby food using fresh fruits and vegetables can be cost-effective compared to buying pre-packaged options.

4. Cloth Diapers: Consider using cloth diapers instead of disposable ones. While there's an initial investment, it can save money in the long run.

5. Budget-Friendly Activities: Look for free or low-cost activities in your community, like library storytimes, local parks, and community events.

6. Generic Brands: Choose generic or store-brand baby products, which are often more affordable than their brand-name counterparts.

7. Plan Meals and Snacks: Preparing meals at home and planning snacks can help avoid unnecessary spending on convenience foods.

8. DIY Crafts and Gifts: Get creative with homemade crafts and gifts for special occasions, saving money while adding a personal touch.

9. Free Educational Resources: Take advantage of free educational resources online or at local libraries for books, games, and learning activities.

10. Hand-Me-Downs: Accept hand-me-downs from friends or family for larger items like strollers, cribs, and high chairs.

11. Family Memberships: If you frequently visit museums, zoos, or other attractions, consider purchasing family memberships, which can often save money in the long term.

12. Minimalist Approach: Embrace a minimalist approach when it comes to baby gear. Focus on essentials to avoid unnecessary spending on items that may not get much use.

13. Group Purchases: Consider joining parenting groups or online communities where members can share bulk purchases or organize group discounts.

Remember, every family's financial situation is unique, so it's essential to find the strategies that work best for your specific circumstances.

CHAPTER 33

COSTS OF OWNING A PET

Having a pet is undoubtedly a source of joy, but it can also be unexpectedly costly. From vet bills to food and grooming, expenses can add up quickly. However, there are several savvy ways to enjoy the companionship of a pet without breaking the bank.

Here are a few simple tips to enjoy having a pet without going broke:

1. Adopt from a Shelter: Adoption fees are generally lower than purchasing from a breeder.

2. Buy Supplies in Bulk: Purchase pet food, treats, and other essentials in bulk to save on per-unit costs.

3. DIY Grooming: Learn to groom your pet at home instead of paying for professional grooming services.

4. Compare Prices: Compare prices for pet medications, grooming services, and vet visits among different providers.

5. Preventive Healthcare: Keep up with your pet's preventive healthcare, including vaccinations and flea/tick preventatives, to avoid costly illnesses.

6. Train at Home: Invest time in training your pet yourself instead of hiring a professional trainer.

7. Buy Affordable Toys: Look for affordable or discounted toys and accessories instead of splurging on expensive ones.

8. Share Toys: Swap or borrow toys with friends who have pets to save money on buying new ones.

9. DIY Toys: Create homemade toys using household items to entertain your pet without spending much.

10. Proper Nutrition: Feed your pet high-quality, balanced food to prevent health issues that could lead to costly vet bills.

11. Regular Exercise: Keep your pet active with regular exercise to maintain their health and reduce the risk of obesity-related health problems.

12. Prevent Accidents: Pet-proof your home to prevent accidents and avoid costly damage to furniture and belongings.

13. Seek Discounts: Look for discounts, coupons, and loyalty programs offered by pet supply stores and veterinary clinics.

14. Use Pet Insurance: Consider investing in pet insurance to help cover unexpected medical expenses.

15. DIY Pet Care: Learn to administer basic medical care, such as trimming nails and cleaning ears, at home to save on vet bills.

With these tips, you can enjoy the awesome company of your furry friend without emptying your wallet.

CHAPTER 34

SAVE ON TRAVEL

Although travel can be enjoyable, it should take a back seat when burdened by debt. The priority should shift to responsible financial management, clearing debts, and building a solid foundation. Delaying travel until financial stability is achieved allows for a stress-free and fulfilling experience without economic concerns. Responsible money management takes precedence over indulging in travel expenses when struggling with debt.

However, if you find yourself needing to travel, these tips can enhance your experience, minimize expenses, and create lasting memories without the stress of overspending. They can help you make the most of your travels without breaking the bank.

BEFORE YOU GO:

1. In Case of Emergency (ICE) Preparations:

    - Carry an ICE paper with essential details in case of an emergency. Keep it on you at all times.

    - Share your travel plans with a trusted friend or family member beforehand.

    - Inform neighbors about your absence and provide contact information for any emergencies.

2. Home Security Measures:

    - Invest in lamp timers to create the illusion of an occupied home.

    - If applicable, arrange for snow plowing and halt newspaper or package deliveries during your absence. Ensure the heat is maintained to prevent frozen pipes, and leave cupboard doors open near pipes.

    - Have a trusted friend or neighbor check on your place during your absence.

3. Travel Planning:

    - Prepare a detailed packing list well in advance to prevent last-minute rushes and avoid forgetting essential items while traveling.

- Bring your own toiletries to avoid the higher costs at hotels or airports.

- Consider taking vitamins or Airborne before your journey to avoid falling sick. Additionally, while airlines are no longer requiring it, wearing a mask and packing hand sanitizer are still recommended precautions.

- Charge your tablet and smartphone fully before leaving. Update your lock screen to include a secondary contact number or email. This way, if you misplace your items, someone can easily reach out to return them to you.

- Enhance suitcase security by adding an AirTag for easy tracking in case of loss. Additionally, attach a luggage tag with your contact details for swift identification and return.

- Remember to include your AirPods or earbuds to enjoy music or watch movies during the trip.

AIRFARE TIPS

1. Smart Booking Practices:

   - Schedule trips at least two weeks in advance for lower fares.

   - Opt for off-season travel to save on flights, hotels, and rental cars.

- Avoid peak travel times and holidays for more affordable fares.

- Compare prices on various travel websites like Expedia, Kayak, and Google Flights.

2. Booking Strategies:

- Consider alternate airports for potentially cheaper options.

- Purchase tickets on Tuesdays, Wednesdays, or Saturdays for better deals. Cheapest flight times are typically in the early morning or late at night.

- Utilize TSA Precheck for a smoother airport experience.

- Beware of hidden fees on budget airlines; a seemingly cheap flight might not include the option to choose your seat or could entail significant charges for checking a bag.

- Check the airline's website and social media for exclusive deals.

3. Flight Comfort and Extras:

- Choose seats strategically based on your preferences.

- Have a light meal before your flight to avoid the possibility of the airline running out of meals when it reaches your aisle or if you're unable to grab a meal during brief layovers in crowded airports. Pack snacks from home.

HOTEL TIPS

1. Booking Accommodations:

   - Use sites like Expedia to compare hotel prices for the destination you plan to visit. Then, check hotel websites for direct booking deals.

   - Read reviews and consider proximity to attractions.

   - Look for hotels offering complimentary breakfast to save on meals.

   - Bundle airfare and hotel or hotel and car rental for potential savings.

   - Consider Airbnb for alternative lodging, but exercise caution. Check the host's rules, as they may stipulate a minimum stay requirement. Be aware that the location might not meet your preferences, the host could cancel, or the property might not match its online portrayal, with no refund recourse.

- Pack light to avoid airline baggage fees; use laundry facilities at the hotel if needed. Stay in hotels near public transportation to cut costs.

- Check loyalty programs for potential perks and discounts.

1. Hotel Safety and Comfort:

- Inspect your hotel room upon arrival for any issues, including lifting the bedding to check for any bugs.

- Stay in well-populated areas, especially if traveling alone.

- Choose accommodations with kitchens or mini-fridges for meal savings.

TRANSPORTATION TIPS

1. Renting a Car:

- Compare rental rates on sites like Expedia or Costco to find the best deal.

- Check your insurance coverage before declining rental agency offers to avoid unnecessary expenses.

- Return the car with a full tank to avoid extra charges for refueling.

2. Using Taxis and Rideshares:

    *   Research average cab fares to avoid overcharging.

    *   Use rideshare services such as Uber or Lyft for cost-effective transportation.

3. Road Trips:

    *   Invest in a road atlas or GPS for navigation.

    *   Pack essentials for road safety, including spare tires and emergency kits.

    *   Plan breaks during long drives to stay alert.

OTHER TRAVEL TIPS

1. General Travel Advice:

    *   Be aware of weather patterns and seasons at your destination.

    *   Pack light to avoid baggage fees and do laundry during longer trips.

    *   Budget for meals, and consider cooking or using coupons to save.

    *   Be cautious when handling valuable belongings in less-populated areas.

- Safeguard against potential theft while exploring. Consider using a secure accessory like a travel pouch to protect the cards and cash you carry on you. Store spare ATM, credit, and identification cards in your hotel safe or suitcase.

- Timeshares may not be ideal if your aim is financial stability.

1. Traveling With Pets:

   - Obtain necessary health certificates and proof of vaccinations.

   - Ensure a smooth journey with your pet by checking and adhering to airline pet policies. Typically, contact the airline to secure a pet-friendly seat, necessitating in-person check-in at least two hours before the flight, as online check-in may not be available.

   - Pack waste bags for your pet's needs during travel.

   - When reserving a pet-friendly room, contact the hotel directly to confirm availability. Some hotels have limited pet-friendly rooms and may be unable to accommodate you if they are unaware of your pet in advance.

2. Timeshares:

- Financial Strain: Exiting timeshare contracts can be legally complex, creating financial challenges.

- Annual Fees: Incurring yearly maintenance fees adds a long-term financial burden.

- Limited Flexibility: Timeshares lack the flexibility needed for changing circumstances or travel preferences.

- High Upfront Costs: Initial expenses for timeshares are typically high, impacting immediate finances.

- Research Complaints: Online complaints highlight common issues, aiding informed decision-making.

3. Staycations:

- Explore local attractions such as parks, zoos, or hidden gems as a tourist in your own town.

- Embrace activities such as hiking or camping in your backyard.

- Create a cozy movie marathon and binge-watch your favorite movies or series.

- Create a Spa Day at home. Pamper yourself with homemade masks, bath salts, and relaxation. Do your nails and pedicures yourself.

- Explore your creative side with DIY craft projects.

- Revisit classic board games or try new ones with family or friends.

Having fun while traveling is great, but if you're dealing with debt, it's essential to prioritize getting your finances in order first. Instead of splurging on trips, focus on paying off your debts and building a strong financial base. Consider staycations as a budget-friendly alternative to traditional vacations. Delaying travel until you're financially solid will ensure you can enjoy future trips without worrying about money troubles. Responsible money management is key, so it's wise to tackle debt before indulging in travel expenses.

CHAPTER 35

RETIREMENT

R etirement looms on everyone's horizon, an inevitable stage of life that demands careful preparation. While individual circumstances vary, there are universal truths about aging, the need to retire, and the importance of financial readiness. This article explores the multifaceted aspects of retirement preparation, emphasizing the significance of debt management, frugality, and savings habits.

Retirement is an inevitable reality; it's not a matter of if but when. The earlier individuals acknowledge and accept this fact, the better positioned they are to navigate the financial intricacies that come with it. Unlike other life events, there's no loan or quick fix for retirement. It requires foresight, discipline, and strategic planning.

DEBT MANAGEMENT

One of the primary hurdles on the path to a secure retirement is debt. Many individuals grapple with loans, credit card balances, and mortgages, often overlooking the long-term impact on their retirement prospects. Debt eats into income, leaving less room for saving and investing. To prepare for retirement, it's essential to embark on a journey of debt reduction.

BUILDING FRUGALITY FOR FUTURE PROSPERITY

Frugality is a powerful ally in retirement planning. Cultivating a mindset of conscious spending and resourcefulness can free up funds for debt repayment and savings. Small, intentional changes in daily habits, like cooking at home or exploring cost-effective entertainment, contribute significantly to long-term financial well-being.

RETIREMENT PLANNING

Once debt is under control and frugal habits are ingrained, the focus shifts to building a robust savings and investment strategy. Retirement accounts, such as 401(k)s or IRAs, become instrumental in creating a financial safety net. The power of compounding, coupled with regular contributions, enhances the growth of retirement funds over the long haul.

Effective Savings and Investment Practices:

1. Automate Contributions: Set up automatic transfers to retirement accounts, ensuring consistent contributions.

2. Diversify Investments: Spread investments across a mix of assets to mitigate risk and optimize returns.

3. Take Advantage of Employer Benefits: Contribute to employer-sponsored retirement plans, especially if the employer offers a matching contribution.

4. Regularly Review and Adjust: Periodically reassess financial goals, risk tolerance, and investment strategies to align with evolving circumstances.

Saving for retirement is paramount, as retirement doesn't come with a loan option. Don't let the idea of pleasing others with excessive spending distract you. Prioritize your financial well-being, ensuring a secure and comfortable retirement. It's like setting up a safety net for yourself, preparing for a time when you won't be working actively. This financial discipline is your ticket to a worry-free future.

Prioritize saving for your retirement over funding your child's college education. While supporting their educational pursuits is commendable, it's not necessary to bear the full financial burden. Many students explore options like grants, scholarships, or student loans. Focus on securing your retirement, as this ensures your financial stability. It's a wise move, considering not all kids finish college, and alternative funding sources are available to support their education.

Retirement planning is not a one-time event but a continuous process. Regular evaluations of financial health, reassessment of goals, and adjustments to the plan are critical components of this dynamic journey. Preparing for retirement requires a holistic approach. Tackling debt, embracing frugality, and consistently saving and investing lay the groundwork for a secure financial future.

Retirement demands intentional steps today for a prosperous tomorrow. By adopting responsible financial habits and planning strategically, individuals can navigate the path to retirement with confidence and enjoy the golden years without financial worries.

CHAPTER 36

MINDSET

Achieving financial freedom is more than a numerical goal; it's an intricate dance between one's mindset and financial actions. A positive mindset, rooted in affirmations, optimism, gratitude, mindfulness, and a learning attitude, becomes a powerful force in overcoming debt and navigating the path to financial independence. Coupled with these elements, perseverance emerges as a key driver, ensuring individuals remain steadfast in their commitment to financial freedom.

THE POWER OF AFFIRMATIONS

Affirmations are not just words; they are catalysts for change. By integrating positive affirmations into daily life, individuals reshape their thoughts and beliefs, fostering an environment conducive to financial success. Affirmations counteract negative self-talk, instilling the belief that overcoming debt and achieving financial freedom are not only possible but inevitable.

Key Affirmations for Financial Freedom:

1. "I am capable of managing my finances wisely."

2. "Every day, I am moving closer to financial independence."

3. "I release all fear and doubt about money, and welcome abundance into my life."

4. "My financial situation does not define my worth; I am deserving of prosperity."

OPTIMISM AS A RESILIENT FORCE

Optimism serves as a potent antidote to financial challenges, providing the resilience needed to face setbacks. An optimistic outlook doesn't negate the reality of debt; instead, it empowers individuals to view obstacles as temporary roadblocks, not insurmountable barriers. Optimists are more likely to take proactive steps, seek solutions, and persevere through financial difficulties.

Practices to Foster Optimism:

1. Focus on Solutions: Channel energy into finding practical solutions rather than dwelling on problems.

2. Celebrate Small Wins: Acknowledge and celebrate every step toward financial goals, no matter how modest.

3. Visualize Success: Create a mental image of financial freedom, reinforcing the belief that it is achievable.

GRATITUDE AS A TRANSFORMATIVE FORCE

Gratitude lays the foundation for a positive mindset. By cultivating gratitude, individuals shift their focus from scarcity to abundance, fostering contentment and hope. Amidst financial challenges, acknowledging and appreciating the positive aspects of life generates a mindset conducive to overcoming debt with perseverance.

Incorporating Gratitude into Daily Life:

1. Gratitude Journal: Regularly jot down aspects of life to be grateful for, fostering a positive perspective.

2. Express Appreciation: Verbally or in writing, express gratitude for the support of loved ones or opportunities.

3. Mindful Reflection: Take moments throughout the day to reflect on positive experiences and express gratitude.

MINDFULNESS AND FINANCIAL DECISION-MAKING

Mindfulness, being fully present in the moment, plays a pivotal role in financial choices. It prevents impulsive spending, promotes informed decisions, and enhances awareness of financial habits. A mindful approach encourages deliberate financial management and resilient responses to challenges.

Practical Mindfulness Strategies:

1. Pause Before Purchasing: Assess whether a non-essential purchase aligns with financial goals before making it.

2. Budget Mindfully: Create a budget reflecting values, ensuring mindful allocation of resources.

3. Regular Financial Check-Ins: Schedule check-ins to assess progress, make adjustments, and reinforce financial goals.

LEARNING AND GROWTH MINDSET

A learning mindset sees challenges as stepping stones to growth. Financial setbacks become lessons, not failures, fostering resilience and adaptability. Embracing a learning attitude promotes continuous education about personal finance, investment, and wealth-building strategies.

Cultivating a Learning Mindset:

1. Financial Education: Actively seek knowledge about personal finance, investment, and wealth-building.

2. Embrace Challenges: Approach financial hurdles as opportunities to learn and grow.

3. Adaptability: Be open to adjusting financial strategies based on lessons learned and changing circumstances.

PERSEVERANCE AS THE DRIVING FORCE

Embedded in every aspect of this transformative journey is perseverance. It is the unwavering commitment to financial freedom despite challenges. Perseverance ensures that individuals never give up, continuing to work diligently to overcome debt and build a secure financial future.

The Role of Perseverance:

1. Never Give Up: Persevere through financial challenges, understanding that setbacks are temporary.

2. Hard Work Pays Off: Keep working diligently to pay off debts and build better financial habits.

3. Stay Committed: Perseverance is the glue that binds positive habits, affirmations, and optimism into lasting financial success.

The Role of Prayer:

Having faith is key in financial matters. Instead of praying for money or a lottery win or what have you, perhaps consider praying for improved financial wisdom and responsibility. Developing positive money habits can lead to long-term financial well-being and success.

Financial freedom demands more than just monetary strategies; it necessitates a resilient mindset. By integrating affirmations, optimism, gratitude, mindfulness, a learning attitude, faith, and, above all, perseverance, individuals empower themselves to navigate the challenges of debt and march confidently toward financial independence. The journey to financial freedom is a marathon, not a sprint, and perseverance ensures that each step taken brings individuals closer to the ultimate goal of financial triumph.

CHAPTER 37

BANKRUPTCY

B ankruptcy is a legal process designed to offer individuals overwhelmed by debt a chance at a financial "fresh start" by canceling certain debts through the intervention of the court. This complex procedure involves a thorough assessment of an individual's financial situation, where a judge and court trustee review assets and liabilities to determine if the debtor genuinely cannot afford to repay their debts. If this is the case, the court may grant a discharge of some debts, giving the debtor relief from the burden of repayment.

THE PROS:

One of the primary advantages of bankruptcy is its ability to halt aggressive creditor actions. Once bankruptcy is filed, an automatic stay is initiated, preventing creditors from making further efforts to collect money from the debtor. This includes putting a stop to property repossession, wage garnishment, and foreclosure on the debtor's home.

However, it's important to note that bankruptcy does not act as a universal eraser of debts. Certain obligations, such as alimony, child support, student loans, and government debts like fines, taxes, or penalties, remain unaffected by the bankruptcy process. Additionally, any substantial purchases made just before filing for bankruptcy, such as cars or boats, may not be discharged.

THE CONS:

Declaring bankruptcy is a significant financial decision with various consequences. One notable drawback is the public nature of the process. When an individual files for bankruptcy, it becomes a matter of public record, potentially affecting their privacy. The procedure itself is not easy to navigate, requiring careful consideration and adherence to legal requirements.

Moreover, bankruptcy comes with financial costs. Legal fees, court filing fees, and other associated expenses can accumulate, further straining an already challenging financial situation. Furthermore, the impact on credit scores is substantial and enduring. A bankruptcy filing can leave a lasting scar on an individual's credit report, making it challenging to secure future loans, rent an apartment, purchase a home, or, in certain circumstances, obtain employment.

Before contemplating bankruptcy, individuals should explore every possible avenue to reduce debts and curtail unnecessary spending. While some might view bankruptcy as the ultimate financial failure, others see it as an opportunity for a "clean slate." There are two main types of bankruptcy for consumers: Chapter 7 and Chapter 13.

Chapter 7 bankruptcy involves the liquidation of assets to pay off debts. However, certain property may be exempt, allowing the individual to retain some possessions. This form of bankruptcy is often referred to as a "straight" or "liquidation" bankruptcy.

Chapter 13 bankruptcy, on the other hand, involves creating a repayment plan to settle debts over a specific period, usually three to five years. This plan allows the debtor to retain their assets while working towards debt discharge.

Given the intricacies of bankruptcy law, it is advisable to delve deeper into the subject and seek guidance from an attorney specializing in bankruptcy. Consulting with a legal professional can provide a clearer understanding of the available options and potential ramifications. Ultimately, bankruptcy should be considered a last resort for those who genuinely feel overwhelmed by insurmountable debt. While it can offer relief, the decision to pursue bankruptcy requires careful consideration of its long-term implications on one's financial health and stability.

CHAPTER 38

TIME

In the pursuit of financial freedom, the tandem of time and discipline emerges as a potent force, especially when navigating the complexities of debt. Thoughtful management of time, coupled with unwavering discipline, can significantly impact your journey to a debt-free and financially secure future. These two elements work synergistically, each enhancing the effectiveness of the other in achieving long-term financial goals.

TIME AND DISCIPLINE

Understanding the symbiotic relationship between time and discipline is pivotal in transforming them into powerful allies on your financial journey. Discipline amplifies the impact of time, ensuring that the moments invested contribute meaningfully to your overarching financial objectives.

Key Insights:

1. Strategic Debt Repayment: Time, when paired with disciplined financial habits, becomes a strategic tool for debt

186

repayment. Consistently allocating specific periods to assess finances, create budgets, and prioritize debt settlement amplifies the effectiveness of your efforts.

2. Discipline Minimizes Procrastination: Procrastination can erode the potential benefits of time. Discipline acts as a counterforce, minimizing procrastination and encouraging consistent action toward financial goals.

STRATEGIC TIME MANAGEMENT AND DISCIPLINED CHOICES

Efficient time management aligns seamlessly with disciplined decision-making, forming the backbone of successful financial strategies. By integrating both aspects, you can optimize your approach to financial challenges and lay the groundwork for enduring financial well-being.

Integrated Strategies:

1. Prioritize Debt Payments: Discipline dictates a structured approach to debt repayment. When combined with intentional time allocation, you create a powerful routine that accelerates progress and cultivates financial discipline.

2. Disciplined Spending Habits: Time spent on evaluating spending habits is maximized through discipline. By adhering to a budget and curbing unnecessary expenses, disciplined financial choices ensure that each moment

dedicated to financial management contributes to your long-term success.

3. Invest in Financial Education: Discipline plays a vital role in enhancing financial literacy. Time invested in learning about personal finance is most effective when coupled with the discipline to apply newfound knowledge to practical financial decisions.

AVOIDING TIME SINKHOLES: DISCIPLINE IN LEISURE ACTIVITIES

Discipline extends beyond financial tasks into leisure activities, safeguarding against time sinkholes that hinder progress. Thoughtful choices in how you spend your free time contribute to both discipline and financial success.

Leisure Discipline:

1. Limiting Excessive Entertainment: Discipline guides the limitation of time spent on television and video games. By adhering to predetermined schedules for leisure, you ensure that these activities remain enjoyable without becoming an impediment to your financial journey.

2. Limit Online Scrolling: Restrict the time spent on aimless internet browsing, checking social media, or playing online games.

3. Strategic Socializing: Discipline in social activities aligns with financial goals. Choosing cost-effective alternatives and planning social engagements thoughtfully reflects disciplined decision-making that supports your broader financial objectives.

Effective time management is pivotal when dealing with debts. Prioritize tasks, create a schedule, and allocate time to debt repayment. Minimize distractions, focus on income-generating activities, and avoid time-consuming habits. Cultivate discipline to ensure each moment contributes to financial progress. Regularly reassess and adjust your time allocation to maintain momentum on the journey to debt freedom. Remember, time is a valuable asset; investing it wisely accelerates your path to financial stability.

CHAPTER 39
FRUGAL HABITS

Changing a habit, especially to become more frugal and get out of debt, can be challenging. However, it's essential for achieving financial stability and securing a debt-free future. Here are some steps to make good habits work for you:

1. Set Clear Goals: Define specific and achievable financial goals, such as paying off debt by a certain date or building an emergency fund. Having clear objectives provides motivation and direction for your frugal habits.

2. Track Your Spending: Monitor your expenses to identify areas where you can cut back and save money. Use budgeting apps or spreadsheets to track your spending habits and identify patterns that may need adjustment.

3. Create a Budget: Develop a realistic budget that outlines your income, expenses, and savings goals. Allocate funds

for essentials like housing, utilities, and groceries while setting aside money for debt repayment and savings.

4. Practice Mindful Spending: Before making a purchase, ask yourself if it aligns with your financial goals and if it's truly necessary. Avoid impulse buying and take time to consider the long-term implications of your spending decisions.

5. Seek Support: Surround yourself with like-minded individuals who support your frugal lifestyle and financial goals. Share tips and strategies with friends or join online communities focused on personal finance and frugality.

6. Celebrate Milestones: Acknowledge and celebrate your progress along the way. Whether it's reaching a savings milestone or paying off a credit card, recognizing your achievements reinforces positive habits and motivates you to continue.

Frugality is not about deprivation but rather about making conscious decisions that align with long-term financial goals. Don't think of frugal as cheap or miserly, but instead, think of it as smart or wealth-minded. Here are 35 frugal habits to save money:

1. Cook meals at home instead of dining out.

2. Pack lunches for work instead of buying them.

3. Use coupons and look for discounts when shopping.

4. Buy generic brands instead of name brands.

5. Cut unnecessary subscriptions and memberships.

6. Cancel cable and opt for streaming services.

7. Use public transportation or carpool instead of driving alone.

8. Walk or bike instead of using a car for short trips.

9. Turn off lights and unplug electronics when not in use to save on electricity bills.

10. Lower the thermostat in winter and use fans instead of air conditioning in summer.

11. Shop at thrift stores and second-hand shops for clothing and household items.

12. Borrow items, such as a ladder, DVDs, cookware, etc., if you can before buying.

13. Use a library card instead of buying books and magazines.

14. Grow your own fruits, vegetables, and herbs at home.

15. DIY home repairs and maintenance whenever possible.

16. Mend clothing instead of replacing it.

17. Host potluck dinners instead of going out to eat with friends.

18. Take advantage of free community events and activities for entertainment.

19. Utilize free resources like public parks and beaches for recreation.

20. Plan meals around weekly grocery store sales and seasonal produce.

21. Don't go grocery shopping while you're hungry. Eat something first.

22. Look over receipts before leaving the store in case of any errors.

23. Buy in bulk for items you frequently use and have storage space for.

24. Utilize leftovers for future meals to minimize food waste.

25. Use less toothpaste, shampoo, dishwasher and laundry detergent.

26. Use bar soap versus facial or body wash. Also, helps cut down on using plastic.

27. Repair or refurbish items instead of buying new ones.

28. Negotiate bills and expenses to get better rates or discounts.

29. Use cash instead of credit cards to avoid overspending.

30. Resist the temptation to browse through magazines or catalogs that arrive in the mail; discard them immediately. Similarly, ignore social media marketing ads by unsubscribing and blocking emails or texts as necessary.

31. Take shorter showers and install water-saving fixtures to reduce water bills.

32. Opt for free or low-cost hobbies and activities instead of expensive ones.

33. DIY gifts and handmade cards for special occasions.

34. Track expenses and regularly review spending habits to identify areas for improvement.

35. Ignore sales such as 30-40% off on items you don't need. Remind yourself it's 100% off if you don't buy it.

Living frugally entails making small yet impactful changes to your daily habits, similar to embarking on a weight loss journey by gradually incorporating healthier choices. These adjustments may include cutting unnecessary expenses, reducing energy consumption, or opting for DIY solutions. While the process of adopting frugality requires time and patience, the rewards are substantial. By embracing a frugal lifestyle, you not only alleviate financial burdens but also cultivate a sense of empowerment and freedom. It's about prioritizing value over extravagance, simplicity over excess, and mindful consumption over impulse buying.

Living frugally allows you to regain control of your finances, pursue your long-term goals, and experience a more fulfilling and sustainable way of life. As you embark on this journey, remember that every small change contributes to significant progress, making the pursuit of frugality both rewarding and worthwhile.

AUTHOR BIO

Kelly Fierce holds a Bachelor's Degree in Business and boasts over two decades of managerial experience in the corporate sector. Her passion for literature and sharing insights on financial matters inspired her to author a book, aiming to enlighten readers about the principles of frugality.

Beyond her professional endeavors, Kelly cherishes spending time with her family amidst the wonders of nature. Whether hiking, fishing, camping, or simply basking in the great outdoors, she finds comfort and rejuvenation in the tranquility of natural surroundings.

Printed in Great Britain
by Amazon

42581963R00109